LONDON
SECRETS

images
Publishing

LOND⊙N
SECRETS

STYLE • DESIGN • GLAMOUR • GARDENS

Text and principal photography by Janelle McCulloch

images
Publishing

Published in Australia in 2017 by
The Images Publishing Group Pty Ltd
ABN 89 059 734 431
6 Bastow Place, Mulgrave, Victoria 3170, Australia
Tel: +61 3 9561 5544 Fax: +61 3 9561 4860
books@imagespublishing.com
www.imagespublishing.com

National Library of Australia Cataloguing-in-Publication entry:

Creator:	McCulloch, Janelle, author.
Title:	London Secrets: Style, Design, Glamour, Gardens / Janelle McCulloch.
ISBN:	9781864706093 (hardback)
Notes:	Includes index.
Subjects:	Architecture—England—London.
	Fashion—England—London.
	Gastronomy—England—London.
	Gardens—England—London.
	London (England)—Description and travel.
	London (England)—Social life and customs.
	London (England)—Guidebooks.
	London (England)—Pictorial works.

Dewey Number: 720.942

Production manager: Rod Gilbert
Senior editor: Gina Tsarouhas
Assisting editor: Helen Koehne
Graphic designers: Nicole Boehringer, Jason Phillips

Printed on 140gsm GoldEast Matt Art paper by Everbest Printing Co. Ltd., in Hong Kong/China

CONTENTS

This page *The dignified façade of Anya Hindmarch's bespoke luggage store in Knightsbridge*
Opposite *The elegant and slightly whimsical entrance of The Pelham hotel in South
Kensington. One of Kit Kemp's first projects, it remains one of London's most beautifully
decorated—and least-known—hotels.*

For my father, Ross Wiedermann, who remains one
of the greatest travellers and adventurers I've ever known.
We will miss your company.

A little note
ON USING THIS GUIDE

Capturing all the hidden corners and secrets of London is a challenge that no book or author could ever hope to meet. And nor should they, because discovering London for yourself and finding your own memorable part of it to call your own is what makes travel magnificent. It is what makes travel memorable.

So, rather than try and list every amazing place in every amazing neighbourhood, this book focuses on a few of the most fascinating places, particularly the lesser-known ones. Many of these are illustrated with photographs and most include websites, so you can research them further if you wish. We've decided to sort them by category or subject matter, just as Mr Dewey would have done, because people are inevitably interested in subjects first, such as bookshops, gardens, design destinations, and so on, rather than in the neighbourhoods where they are located.

There's also an emphasis on design, decoration and gardens and botanical spaces, rather than fashion, because the latter has been extensively covered in other guides. (And those books have covered the subject far better than I could have done!) There's a small amount of fashion in the last chapters, including some secret vintage couture sources and a few must-see destinations—I felt that some London places were too memorable and beautiful not to include—but by and large the places featured here are those that aren't widely publicised. They're places that will show you London in a new light, and give you a new perspective on the city.

I hope you find as much inspiration in this city as I and others have done over the years. Whether you're here for a a few days, a week, a month or a year, I hope you have a wonderful time!

Janelle McCulloch

INTRODUCTION

Hogarthian tea rooms and sleek design hotels; enchanting emporiums of lovely clutter and elegant, understated new restaurants; old-fashioned stores with polished mahogany counters and sophisticated boutiques with glamorous brass fittings; grand royal palaces and tiny secondhand bookshops; great museums and glorious pubs; City boys in Paul Smith and Chelsea girls in Joseph and Issa; taxi drivers who are versed in politics and poetry and antiques dealers so adept they can recognise a fake at 50 paces … London is a dichotomy of contrasts—dramatic and yet discreet, edgy and yet built on heritage brands, and of course noticably bohemian and yet still very, very British—that has endeared itself to visitors for decades. It is a city of unparalleled loveliness, particularly in June, when the fleeting summer season sees the city erupt with flowers, festivals, parties and *joie de vivre*. But London is also a mystery in many respects. Like the British people, it likes to remain a little reserved. It's not the 'done thing', after all, to show everything at once. Vegas, this is not.

But if you can slip past the formal façades (of both the buildings and the people), you'll be rewarded with spaces, places and characters that will charm and delight. In fact, some of London's most memorable destinations are behind its closed doors, off its main streets and down its enthralling Dickensian lanes. Cecil Court, for example, is home to a line of irresistibly atmospheric bookshops and print stores harbouring a wealth of signed first editions. Regent's Park hides a secret rose garden—Queen Mary's Rose Garden, which shelters 12,000 roses that provide a scent along the paths in the summer months. The National Portrait Gallery—one of the country's most magnificent galleries—doesn't publicise that one of London's best views is from its top-floor restaurant. Some of the V&A's (Victoria and Albert Museum's) most beautiful pieces are not in its galleries and exhibitions in South Kensington but in its archives at the Clothworkers' Centre at Blythe House, where tours are run on the last Friday of every month (the venue may be changing in early 2017). And some of the most delightful afternoon teas are not in the grand old salons of Piccadilly and Knightsbridge but in the rustic, leafy garden nurseries of Maida Vale and Richmond.

These are the parts of London that most travellers—and locals—rarely see: the London of curiosities and eccentricities, of creativity and quirkiness, of secret surprises and unexpected charms.

And then, of course, there are all the bright, shiny, boldly ambitious new destinations, ranging from restaurants such as Spring to hotels such as Ham Yard, not to mention all the edgy, innovative new galleries, bars, riverside paths, pubs, and other exciting projects punctuating the city's landscape. There is so much happening in London it's not surprising that the city has become the most popular tourist destination in the world, according to MasterCard's Global Destination Cities Index.

But lest you think that London is losing its character under all the new layers of development, architecture, ideas and entrepreneurialism, don't worry: the old-fashioned courtesy is still clearly there. Despite the changes to the skyline and streets, London remains a city of dignity and civility, of graciousness and charm. Spend a week here and you'll remember what real manners are.

The problem is: how do you find the loveliest and most memorable corners of this creative, inspirational metropolis? How do you hunt down the sartorial, style and design treasures without knowing an insider or a savvy local who's generous with their recommendations? Well, we've done the hard yards for you. Here, in this illustrated guide to this very grand city, are hundreds of beautiful places and distinctive destinations that will assist you to discover London anew.

So fix yourself a cup of proper English tea and join me as I explore this very dignified but very daring town, which continues to beguile and delight, even after all these years. Gracious, glamorous and spectacularly memorable, but still, thankfully, utterly indefatigable, London is lovelier than ever. I hope this book inspires you to visit it again soon.

"London is also a mystery in many respects. Like the British, it likes to remain a little reserved."

A FEW FANTASTIC DESIGN FESTIVALS AND EVENTS

12 **DECORATIVE ANTIQUE AND TEXTILES FAIR (January / April / September)** The Decorative Antiques and Textiles Fair takes place three times a year in Battersea Park. The fair is well worth going to if you happen to be in town. Dealers from all over London, as well as the rest of the country, set up stands stocked with beautiful antique furniture and textiles.

www.decorativefair.com

CHELSEA FLOWER SHOW (May) The horticultural mecca that is the Chelsea Flower Show seems to take over Chelsea, if not the whole of London, for five days in May. It's put on by the Royal Horticultural Society (RHS) in the grounds of the Royal Hospital Chelsea, and it is arguably the most famous flower show in the United Kingdom, and perhaps in the world. Highlights include the grand Show Gardens designed by leading names (with heavy backing by major brands), the Floral Marquee in the centre of the event, and smaller gardens such as the Artisan and Urban Gardens. It's expensive, but if you buy a half-day ticket, it's more reasonable.

www.rhs.org.uk/shows-events/rhs-chelsea-flower-show

CHELSEA IN BLOOM (May) Staged to coincide with the Chelsea Flower Show, Chelsea in Bloom encourages retailers in the Sloane Square and Chelsea area to adorn their windows and stores with botany and flowers using imaginative, horticultural-themed displays. Those participating are then judged by an expert panel of judges from the Chelsea Flower Show. A map is posted on the website just prior to the Chelsea Flower Show so people can wander from one to the other and sigh away, or there are (free) walking tours of the windows with a Chelsea in Bloom guide several times a day. The windows are always, always amazing. Don't miss Kate Spade's displays: last year it was a jungle theme, with giant flamingos made out of fresh pink and red carnations. There's also Pimlico in Bloom and Belgravia in Bloom.

www.chelseainbloom.co.uk

CHELSEA FRINGE FESTIVAL (May / June) Entirely independent of the RHS Chelsea Flower Show, though acting with its support, and run as a kind of symbiotic event at the same time, this is a three-week, garden-focused festival that has become almost as famous as Chelsea itself. There are events and experiences, exhibits, talks and walks.

www.chelseafringe.com

GROW LONDON GARDEN FAIR (June) Yet another garden festival that's 'grown' off the back of the hugely popular Chelsea Flower Show, this garden fair is staged on Hampstead Heath, which is the perfect place for it. There are more than 100 producers of furniture, accessories and rare flowers and plants, plus free talks from top names (last year featured Sarah Raven, Fergus Garrett and Thomas Broom of Petersham Nurseries, who talked about edible flowers). You can also sit down with a professional garden designer for 20 minutes to get advice for your own plot.

www.growlondon.com/london

ARTISTS AT HOME (June) An inspiring idea initiated by the artistic community of riverside Chiswick and Hammersmith, this annual event sees dozens of artists open their doors for a summer's weekend in June. Art lovers and those who'd love to be artists or crafts people are invited to meet the artists in their own studios, chat about their work and perhaps buy a piece or two. Anybody who has been in a painting studio or a potter's workshop knows how wonderful these spaces are. Now multiply the experience by 20 and you can see what a wonderful weekend this is!

www.artistsisathome.net

OPEN GARDEN SQUARES WEEKEND (June) Open Garden Squares allows people to peek behind the gates of more than 200 gardens that wouldn't normally be open to the public. All for just £10 for the whole weekend. There are gardens on barges, on rooftops, in restaurants, hidden behind historic buildings, in artists' studios and galleries, beyond the gates of community gardens, and in many of the private London squares that are usually locked.

www.opensquares.org

LONDON FESTIVAL OF ARCHITECTURE (June) The London Festival of Architecture is a month-long program of events and activities held in June, focusing on the importance of architecture and design in London. It is organised by three partners: New London Architecture, The Architecture Foundation and The Royal Institute of British Architects, in conjunction with other leading cultural and academic institutions, architects, engineers, designers and artists. There are exhibitions and installations, talks and debates, open studios, tours, family activities, film screenings, student shows and architecture evenings.

www.londonfestivalofarchitecture.org

LONDON DESIGN FESTIVAL (September) The London Design Festival runs for nine days in September each year, celebrating the city's creativity and design community. The program of events usually features some of the country's greatest designers, thinkers, practitioners, retailers and educators. The festival has become a significant event in the London calendar, with more than 350,000 visitors from more than 60 countries. The annual program usually involves more than three hundred events and projects staged by 300 partner organisations.

www.londondesignfestival.com

OPEN HOUSE LONDON (September) Open House London's mission is to promote an appreciation of architecture. It is best known for its annual Open House Weekend, which is a two-day event held on one weekend each September. The event is the London version of the European Heritage Days (Journées Européennes du Patrimoine), a Europe-wide event that started in France in 1983. During the Open House Weekend many buildings considered to be of architectural significance open their doors for free public tours. Well-known buildings that are usually closed to the public but are often open on Open House Weekend include Marlborough House, Lancaster House, Mansion House, the Foreign and Commonwealth Office, and Horse Guards. It is often possible to turn up and go straight into some establishments, although queues are an hour or two long at the most popular buildings, while in other cases admission is by advance booking of a guided tour only.

www.openhouse.org.uk

LONDON VINTAGE FASHION, TEXTILES AND ACCESSORIES FAIR (Every four to five weeks) Designers, decorators, fashion addicts, boutique owners and collectors regularly head down to Hammersmith Town Hall for a one-day fair of fashion and textiles. It's a highly regarded event that draws top dealers and serious buyers, with the finds ranging from 1800 vintage to 1980 fashion pieces. There are couture gowns, 1950s handbags, vintage fabrics, monogrammed luggage and accessories galore. Note: The serious buyers get there early—by 8am—to nab the best stuff.

www.pa-antiques.co.uk/londonvintagefashionfair.html

"You can find inspiration in everything. And if you can't, look again."

—London fashion designer **Paul Smith**

"There's nowhere else like London. Nothing at all, anywhere."

—Fashion designer **Vivienne Westwood**

This page *The Wolseley, a former Art Deco auto showroom; now one of the most popular bistros in town* **Opposite** *Trafalgar Square*

24 (STYLISH) HOURS IN LONDON

Aim to schedule your visit for the last Friday on the month. (The reason will become clear in a moment.) Book into either The Pelham hotel (one of Kit Kemp's first hotel designs and still a fabric-lover's delight) near the V&A (Victoria and Albert Museum) or one of the flamboyant suites at Blakes, which offer a fantasy of textiles, antiques and unusual design ideas. Blakes was one of the world's first 'boutique' hotels and still offers an inimitable experience, especially for design fans. It remains a favourite of many hotel experts, including the founder of cult hotel-booking site Mr and Mrs Smith and the founder of LUXE Guides Grant Thatcher. Begin the day with a tour of either the magnificent galleries and design exhibitions of the nearby V&A or the V&A's enormous and utterly memorable costume archives, stored at the Clothworkers' Centre at Blythe House in West Kensington. Get up and close with vintage Dior, Chanel and more. (Last Friday of every month only, which is why you need to time your stay accordingly if you want to see it.) Wander back to Kensington, popping into the opulent Leighton House on the way to see the extraordinary blue salon, decorated with 1000 peacock-blue tiles collected from demolished mansions in Iran and Syria on the owner's Grand Tour trips. Then head north through Kensington Gardens (peek into the pretty Sunken Garden on the way) until you reach Notting Hill and the Portobello Road markets. Fridays are quieter and you'll be able to browse the stalls in peace without tourists poking you in the ribs for an Instagram. Don't miss the hidden stalls selling antique silverware (often bought from great country estates), and the side streets full of intriguing design stores, including the Lacy Gallery, a glorious ode to vintage and antique picture frames, most of them ex-museum pieces. (Notting Hill's best stores will be discussed in the following pages.) Grab the tube a few stops to Baker Street for a wander through the scented and still somewhat secret (at least to tourists) flower beds of Queen Mary's Rose Garden in Regent's Park. Then it's just a short walk south to the beautifully restored, Grade II–listed Victorian-Gothic building, the Chiltern Firehouse hotel, for a late lunch in the stylish garden or parlour. Head around the corner to Marylebone High Street for seriously stylish shopping (don't miss Designers Guild, Daunt Books, Marlene Birger and the ribbons and trims of VV Rouleaux). Then pootle over to Liberty's department store for gorgeous labels in a grand, quintessentially British setting. Make sure you visit the scarf department and the vintage designer corners—glam couture galore. If you love fabrics, don't miss the nearby textile stores of Berwick Street and Dean Street. You may need a pick-me-up drink at this point, so stop in either the National Portrait Gallery's top-floor restaurant (amazing views over London), or the whimsical spaces of Sketch (try the all-pink Gallery dining space by Paris-based designer India Mahdavi) or the Wolseley on Piccadilly, a former Art Deco auto showroom that's now one of London's most glamorous bistros. If you're right to press on, meander into Mayfair. Having gone through an urban facelift in recent years, the village is once again strutting its stuff, with new boutiques, hotels and hideaways galore. Don't miss the Dover Street Market, an unusual, multilevel fashion retail and concept store created by Rei Kawakubo of Japanese fashion label Comme des Garçons. It stocks the best in contemporary fashion labels. There are many other beautiful stores in this area, from bespoke to cool and edgy, to places that have been there for generations. If you're in the mood for more art, check out the exhibitions at the Royal Academy. Or if you prefer books, pop by Heywood Hill for priceless first editions and lovely new biographies, or Assouline's grand new store (set in a converted grand bank) for enormous tomes on fashion and design. Then it's time to get ready for dinner. Congratulations! You've packed a lot of London into a little day!

Opposite clockwise from top *The River Thames and London Eye at twilight; David Collins Studio's glamorous interior design for the Artesian bar, which won an award for the Best Bar in the World; one of the many beautiful exhibitions at the V&A, this one was on the photographs of Richard Avedon*

This page clockwise from top left *Liberty department store, one of the most glamorous and enthralling stores in London; the Lacy Gallery in Notting Hill, a 'gallery' of glorious antique picture frames; the view over Big Ben, Trafalgar Square and London Eye from the top-floor restaurant of the National Portrait Gallery*

18

From left to right *A quintessential British tailor in Bloomsbury; the tiny Dove pub on the River Thames in Chiswick; The Wolseley on Piccadilly, during a busy lunch session*

20

NEW CHANGES TO THE LONDON LANDSCAPE

In recent years, London has been coming out from behind its famously dignified, decorous character and has begun behaving with a little more rebellion. Gone is the British reserve and restraint and in its place is a daring, dazzling ambition with a no-holding-back philosophy. It's almost as if the English eccentricity and eclecticism that's been kept in check all these years (it's often glimpsed but has never been mainstream) has become not just acceptable but expected of people. Creativity is now the new currency. Energy is the new default setting.

This new pace is, as you would expect, having an affect on the city, in many different ways. As the Creative Class charges forward, the London landscape is changing in its wake. Extraordinary projects are being planned, funded, approved and built, and London feels livelier as a result, as if the spring season has descended on the place and never left. While many of these new projects have their detractors, by and large the changes to the city have been a good thing, if only because they're igniting renewed interest from international visitors. In fact, according to the annual MasterCard Global Destinations Cities Index, which provides a ranking of the 132 most visited cities around the world, the city has recently overtaken New York, Paris and Bangkok as the number-one travel destination in the world, with more than 18 million visitors and a predicted increase in that number this year.

London is again having its day. And no matter how you see the new changes to the city and its architecture and street scenes, that is indeed a good thing.

NEW PROJECTS TO KEEP AN EYE ON

ALAIN DE BOTTON'S PHILOSOPHER'S HOTEL When the bestselling author of *The Architecture of Happiness* and other titles put forward plans for a thinking-person's hideaway in Hampstead, the locals rose up with their (very polite) arms. "Completely unacceptable" was one comment. Nevertheless, Camden Council approved the project. Some of the rooms planned include 'Keats' Living Room', 'Freud's Study', and 'Constable's Studio'. No word yet on when the hotel will open.

HOTEL COSTES This hotel may have opened by the time this book is published, but at the time of writing it is still in the process of being built. Whenever it opens, it is set to be as popular as its sister hotel in Paris, the Hôtel Costes, which is a magnet for glamorous types who fly in and out for Paris Fashion Weeks and other super-stylish soirees. The Paris version has been described as a "sexy velvet boudoir" where beautiful people flock for "lounging, posing, and listening to music". It's not known whether the London version will be done in the same opulent, decadent way, but it will likely be the same designer—Jacques Garcia—who does it, and he's not known for minimalism. Set to open on Sloane Square in Chelsea.

Above *Queen's Walk along the southern bank of the River Thames*

PERSONAL FAVOURITES

ANTIQUES HUNTING London has some of the best antiques, second-hand and vintage stores in the world. From couture to jewellery, silverware to chairs, there is always something in London that will make you stop, turn, and ponder the beauty and craftsmanship of those glorious and elaborately decorative pieces. Some of London's best sources of covetable antiques and vintage items are Bentleys (204 Walton Street) for elegant old trunks and luggage (amongst other things); Henry Gregory (82 Portobello Road) for lovely old pieces in leather, silver and other precious materials; Raker UK in the Bourbon Hanby Arcade (151 Sydney Street)—the arcade is itself a great secret—for amazing Louis Vuitton trunks, hat boxes, steamer bags and other exquisite leather bags, plus more items by Hermès, Cartier, Asprey and Tiffany; and Barham Antiques (83 Portobello Road) for gorgeous antique boxes in silver, etched glass, polished timber and brass. My favourite silver shops are also on Portobello Road: Atlam (111 Portobello Road) is full of polished trays, candlesticks, platters, teapots, boxes and other pretty things, while nearby there is a secret silver dealer tucked down a tiny lane that always offers huge discounts on Edwardian, Victorian and other antique silver trays that look exactly like the kind Ralph Lauren sells for 10 times as much. I never remember the name, but head for the cluster of silver shops in this part of Portobello Road, and look for a little passage that's stacked with silver—it's even hanging from the ceiling and walls.

ARCHITECTURE TOURS It can be difficult to get a handle on modern London, especially when it's changing so dramatically and rapidly. Fortunately, there are fantastic architecture tours offered by Open-City London. Go by boat down the Thames to see the iconic landmarks (new and old) from the great vantage point offered by being on the water, or do a walking tour, an evening tour, a photography tour, even an architecture tour by bike!

www.open-city.org.uk

TEXTILE SHOPPING Londoners have always had a love of textiles. They are possibly the most talented textile designers in the world, next to the French and the Indians. Combine this passion with their love of colour, texture (velvet and wool are very big in this country!) and embroidery, and you get some of the most tactile and sophisticated must-have fabrics in the textile world. I never—never—miss a visit to Designers Guild on King's Road, and if I lived in London all year long (still a wish), I'd be first in line at the Colefax and Fowler sale in January. As it is, there's enough to keep a fabric lover occupied for days in London, especially at the Chelsea Harbour Design Centre, which combines 100 fabric and textile showrooms with one great design bookshop. Pure bliss!

Vanity Fair magazine called it "the design world's mecca", and it's not an exaggeration. Allow several hours for browsing.

THE ISABELLA PLANTATION IN RICHMOND PARK If you're overwhelmed with London, or just seeking a leafy space to escape the city for a short while, the 16 hectares (40 acres) of woodland glades in the Isabella Plantation are a glorious place to wander on a sunny day, especially in late April or May when the 100 different varieties of azaleas are in bloom. To reach Richmond Park, hop aboard one of the Thames River Boats (www.thamesriverboats.co.uk) from Westminster, which takes you past some of the most iconic buildings in London. (The pier is next to Westminster Bridge, opposite the the Palace of Westminster / Houses of Parliament.) Or you can walk from Richmond station. The Plantation features enormous trees and exotic flowers, and normally has something in bloom at any time of the year, although late April / early May is perhaps the best time to see the sea of mauve and pink azaleas.

WILLIAM VINTAGE William Vintage is the Didier Ludot of London. If you're not sure who Didier Ludot is, then this place probably isn't for you, so don't worry about it. But if you're a fan of vintage couture and glamorous gowns from the 1920s to the 1970s, you will absolutely love this store. Victoria Beckham, Tilda Swinton, Lily Allen and Gillian Anderson are all fans, and if it should seem like there should be more celebrities on the client list, that's probably because all the others haven't discovered it yet. It's hidden away in the shoppers' oasis that is Marylebone, and offers some of the most beautiful fashion imaginable. Forget the pieces you find on the nearby streets (or on Net-a-Porter); these are one-offs you'll want to buy and keep forever. A 1950s Balenciaga gown that looks so pristine it could be from 2015. A rare Madame Gres that would make a great party dress. Vintage Balmain, Dior New Look, and YSL (before it became Saint Laurent), including a coveted Le Smoking jacket … it's like unearthing trunk upon glorious trunk of couture in your wealthy granny's attic, if she's the kind of granny who lives in Chatsworth or Paris. Owned by William Banks-Blaney, who is as nice as pie, it's an authentic treasure trove that's relished by collectors as much as business women looking for something different to impress their board members or clients. And many of the pieces are museum-worthy. One client bought a 1924 Chanel ribbon dress for £9000, which was so rare that Chanel offered to buy it from her for twice the price. William Banks-Blaney works with at least 15 fashion houses on their archives; his knowledge of couture and fashion labels is incredible. Pop in for a browse or to buy something truly special. You won't regret it, especially when you're still wearing it 20 years later.

TOURIST TRAPS
THAT ARE STILL WORTH SEEING

THE LONDON EYE The route to reach it—across Westminster Bridge and along the Thames waterfront—is almost as pretty as the sweeping vistas over London from the Eye itself.

CHURCHILL'S BUNKER Churchill's secret World War II underground bunker is still intriguing, even after all these years.

KENSINGTON GARDENS A real joy in summer when the profusion of trees and lawn areas offer shade and tranquillity and a rest from traipsing around London, while the people- and dog-watching offer entertaining distractions.

BUCKINGHAM PALACE The best way to reach it is to walk through St James Park or down the Mall; both offer classic London views that have remained unchanged for decades.

PRIMROSE HILL A beautiful park, with one of the best views of London.

COLUMBIA ROAD FLOWER MARKETS Although London's 'official' flower market is the New Covent Garden Markets—which has moved south of the river between Vauxhall and Battersea, the smaller, more intimate flower market on Columbia Road is an atmospheric escape on a Sunday morning, when the New Covent Garden is closed. Look for the geranium stall; it's so popular the crowd is often five deep around it. Great fashion and garden boutiques, and cafés here, too.

PORTOBELLO ROAD This place flat-lined for a few years, but seems to have renewed energy (and popularity) again. A great tip is to avoid it on Saturdays, when the crowds make browsing impossible, and opt instead for Friday. Some of the stalls aren't open, but there's still enough to see and shop, and not nearly as many people in the way.

SURPRISING NEIGHBOURHOODS TO SEEK OUT AND EXPLORE

Sometimes London can be overwhelming. The intensity of Regents Street and Oxford Street alone can leave you reeling. When the pace becomes too much, retreat to some of the quieter, more bucolic suburbs and neighbourhoods, such as **Richmond**, **Chiswick**, and the riverside villages of the south, which almost look like something from the country. In **Barnes High Street**, the atmosphere is straight out of a charming, 1950s, semi-rural London. Parts of **Chiswick**, too, still feel as they did years ago, when the area was mostly fields and artists' weekenders. (JMW Turner and William Morris both had country homes here, among others.) There are many lovely riverfront pubs in Chiswick, which are wonderful for a drink or lunch after a long walk along the Thames. (The tiny Dove pub on the river is very cute.) One of my favourite riverside walks is from

the Royal Botanic Gardens in Kew (don't miss the famous Palm House) down to Richmond and then across the fields to Petersham Nurseries for lunch. It's pure bliss on a warm spring weekend.

If you happen to be in **Chelsea**, whether for the Chelsea Flower Show or just a spot of textile or fashion shopping, don't assume the best bits are concentrated around Sloane Square and King's Road. Some of the most beautiful streets in this neighbourhood are around **Cheyne Walk**, where the historic houses have been home to many artistic and literary figures over the years (more in this book). The **Chelsea Physic Garden** in this same area offers a pocket of horticultural loveliness—and a great insight into plants and their medicinal qualities.

A few steps north of Chelsea is **Knightsbridge**, which many people think is just Harrods, Harvey Nichols and a whole lot of intimidating rich people. But in fact the tiny streets hidden behind Cheval Place are some of the prettiest in London. Walk down Montpelier Street (look for the pretty pink cottage on the right), then turn left at either **Cheval Place or Montpelier Place** and look for the secret gate in the old brick wall on Rutland Street, which leads to **Rutland Mews**. From then you can walk down the lovely **Ennismore Street** to the secret garden behind the Oratory or keep exploring the streets to the north, feeling a twinge of envy for the people lucky enough to live here. (There are marvellous designer resale boutiques in Cheval Place too; the rumour is Diana used to leave her unwanted clothes at Pandora.)

Nearby, in the area around **Gloucester Road**, some of the most photogenics mews cottages in London are to be found down **Kynance Mews,** which is a garden-lover's dream in spring when the wisteria trailing above the doorways breaks into racemes of purple flowers. In fact, there are so many mews streets and lanes around here that you could almost weave your way from Earl's Court to Kensington Gardens without going out on a main road. **Launceston Place** in this same area is also a picturesque street of charming houses and gardens: don't miss the tiny village-within-a-village at the northern end of the street (look for the elegant navy-blue façade of Launceston Place restaurant). Who would have thought that such a pastoral scene could be found a few steps south of the bustling Kensington High Street?

And of course **Notting Hill** is as famous for its hidden corners as its charming thoroughfares. I love stumbling across the small architectural treasures here—particularly the candy-coloured Victorian villas and doors that are painted sky blue, lavender, peach, even bougainvillea pink. (Not surprisingly, the annual Carnival here is one of the most colourful in Europe.) You have to keep your eyes peeled for the best houses, as they're often the smallest. One day, I noticed the charming cottage that belongs to the gardener of Ladbroke Square Garden (found on Kensington Park Road to the right of the garden; marked by a plaque saying simply 'cottage'). Another time I spotted a hot-pink house with gilt door handles and a front plaque that simply stated the words 'Bank Robber'. (Located at 52 Lonsdale Road; it's actually the home of the gallerist who owns the BANKROBBER gallery inside.) You could walk for hours through Notting Hill and not tire of the colour, life and character in the streetscenes.

On the other side of town, **Spitalfields** is just as much of a surprise. Centuries ago, this area was the site of the medieval priory of St Mary Spital (Hospital), hence the name, Spitalfields. (Part of the brickwork of the priory survives in the basement of a building.) Later, it became the bustling hub for the silk-weaving industry after Protestant refugees expelled from Catholic France congregated here, creating a quality of silk cloth that was almost as famous as that of Lyons. Today, it's a lively, intriguing part of London that's been rediscovered by artists (Travey Emin lives here), musicians, writers and other creatives who love its quirky nature and eclectic, bohemian-meets-edgy boutiques. There are some great restaurants and fantastic shops here, but the best thing to do is a walking tour (there are many advertised on the internet), in order to better understand the wonderful history of this fascinating area.

To the south, lies the rapidly changing (some say gentrifying) neighbourood of **Brixton**. Once fiercely multicultural but now multi-everything, this eclectic village is a hymn to the new creative class seeking cheaper office space and housing away from prohibitively priced inner-city London. The 1930s Granville Arcade on Atlantic Road in Brixton Village has been restored and revitalised in the past few years, while the village itself offers all kinds of restaurants and shops to suit all kinds of tastes. The overwhelming feeling here is one of bright colours, high energy and good vibes.

To the north lies the Arcadian idyll of **Hampstead,** more countryside than capital, where you can wander along peaceful streets and past exquisite 18th-century manor houses, or down small cobblestone lanes leading demurely to old churches and flowery churchyards. There's also Hampstead Heath and its 324 hectares (800 acres) of untamed woodland, with sweeping views back over London. Despite the fame of Hampstead, there are many lesser-known parts to it, from the wonderful, well-stocked second-hand bookstore Keith Fawkes (on Flask Walk, just around the corner from the tube station; look for the Kelly-green façade) to Well Walk, one of the prettiest streets in Hampstead.

But if you want to really get off the beaten track, try nearby **Highgate**, home to some of the most atmospheric architecture and streets in London. Take the rambling, part-timbered pub the Gatehouse, for example, which is named after the gateway where travellers once paid tolls to cross the Bishop of London's lands. (It was this 'high gate' that gave the village its name.) The walls are adorned with prints and photographs of bygone Highgate; a mesmerising gallery of history. Nearby, sprawled across 7 hectares (17 acres) and looking like a Hollywood film set with its ivy-clad railings and leaning stone tombs is **Highgate Cemetery**, once ruinous then enthusiastically restored in the 1980s. The cemetery is notable for both the people buried there as well as for its unofficial status as a fantastic place to explore history and nature in equal measure. The eastern part contains the graves of people such as Charles Dickens, George Eliot and Karl Marx, but it's the older, western part you really want to see for its impressive collection of Victorian mausoleums, gravestones and elaborately carved tombs, which can only be visited on tours. The two cemetery grounds are full of trees and wildflowers; don't miss the Circle of Lebanon topped by a huge Cedar of Lebanon, and wonderful leafy, winding paths through tombs and vaults. It may seem morbid and eerie, but it's actually surprisingly beautiful. Clearly a serene place to be buried.

Read on for more neighbourhood delights in the chapters to come.

From opposite left to right *A botanical sculpture on Palace Gate near Gloucester Road reflects the greenery of nearby Kensington Gardens; a pretty cottage on Canning Place (in the same area) becomes a purple poem in spring, thanks to the racemes of wisteria; the delightful Kynance Place is a painting in the afternoon sun; the charming entrance to Kynance Mews (which runs parallel to Kynance Place) is as enticing as the passageway itself*

This page and opposite *Brushfield Street and the surrounding lanes and passages in Spitalfields offer a snapshot of 'old London', with exquisitely old-fashioned delis like Verde and Co to shops such as A. Gold, a former French milliner that is now a fantastic food store*

This page and opposite *The streets of Notting Hill reflect the creativity of both the media /
fashion professionals who live there and their Caribbean neighbours, who were there long before
the cool crowd moved in (and in fact made the area cool to begin with!). Some streets look like
mini Jamaicas, with houses painted in bold shades of bougainvillea pink, tangerine and pineapple
yellow. Others are (slightly) more subdued, with hues of navy blue and cobalt, but are no less
charming. Even some of the cars are colour coordinated to match.*
Following pages from left to right *The Somerset House; William Morris fabric; a lantern in
Notting Hill; the extraordinary Soane Museum; a detail of notes from the V&A*

ALL THE STRAN
CAME TODAY

Appraised within th
white walls of the s
and with only a hor
plane for balance, V
subjects face the le
carefully arranged
His intention is to e
artifice – though it'
inclination hard to
in favour of clarity
perhaps to scrutinis
sitter's idiosyncrasie
a taxonomer might
recently harvested s

AN ABBREVIATED LIST OF SOME OF LONDON'S BEST DESIGN SECRETS

18 STAFFORD TERRACE (LINLEY SAMBOURNE HOUSE) You'd never guess that the beautiful but rather nondescript façade of this Holland Park residence hides one of the best stories of preservation in London's history; one that curiously mixes Antony Armstrong-Jones' family (the former husband of Princess Margaret) with a *Punch* cartoonist and a wealthy stockbroker. How? Well, it all began in the late 1800s when *Punch* cartoonist Edward Linley Sambourne married Marion Herapath, the daughter of a wealthy stockbroker. The couple paid £2000 for an 89-year lease on 18 Stafford Terrace using funds from Marion's father, and set about redecorating the house in the fashionable 'aesthetic' or artistic style of the period. This included elegant William Morris wallpapers, collections of blue-and-white Chinese porcelain, exquisite prints and paintings and elaborate stained-glass windows. All very decadent. All very Victorian. When Edward and Marion died within a few years of each other, their son inherited it, and when he died in 1946, it went to his sister. However, she already had grand houses in London and the country. So what to do with it? Well, she wanted to keep it—it did, after all, have great sentimental value—so she persuaded her daughter Anne to use it as a *pied à terre*. Anne by then had married Ronald Armstrong-Jones in 1925, and they had a son Antony, who would later marry Princess Margaret in 1960 and become the Earl of Snowdon. (Are you keeping up? It's convoluted, I know.) When the Snowdons divorced (the parents, not Princess Margaret and Antony), Anne married Michael, sixth Earl of Rosse. By this time, none of the family lived in the house, but they still felt sentimental about its glorious interiors, art and architecture. So, after a lengthy process in which the house was passed from one society to the other, it was eventually bought by the Royal Borough of Kensington and Chelsea. And it is now one of the most interesting design destinations in London; a startling insight into Victorian grandeur. Several films have been set here, including Merchant Ivory's *A Room with a View*, and the recent BBC drama *Life in Squares*, which centered on the lives and loves of the Bloomsbury Group. If you love interior design, and particularly the William Morris style of patterning and decorating, which is now fashionable again, this is a must-see. Although you can walk around on your own, try to do a guided tour, which explains the furniture, the décor, the family and their personalities. (See also page 108.)

19 PRINCELET STREET Few people know about this architectural gem, probably because it's rarely open to the public. But if you can rustle up a small group, it does allow tours through, or you can wait for an Open Day, which is scheduled a few times a year. (The building is raising funds so it can open permanently in future. See its website for more details.) It's a Grade II–listed, unrestored, Huguenot silk-merchant's home in Spitalfields that dates from 1719. It was originally the home of the Ogier family, who escaped from persecution in France and entered the silk-weaving trade in London. They prospered and this home was the result of their success. But then, as many of the Huguenots moved away from the area, this and other elegant Georgian houses in this area were subdivided into lodgings and workshops. (Even the attic windows of this residence were altered to let in more light for weavers to work). Successive owners then used it for various trades: Mary Ellen Hawkins used it as an industrial school, while Isaiah Woodcock used it for his carving and gilding work. Today, 19 Princelet Street in Spitalfields is not only one of London's most unusual historic buildings, but a fascinating link to life in London during the 18th and 19th centuries. Beyond the shabby front doors are secrets and suitcases, poems and stories, peeling walls and romantically ruinous spaces. As a tribute to the Huguenots, it has been loosely converted to a museum of immigration and diversity in Europe. (It's still rather rustic.) But its real beauty is in giving us a glimpse into how people lived, worked, assimilated and prospered in the past.

www.19princeletstreet.org

5 WANDSWORTH ROAD A National Trust secret, this is a sublime little house. It was owned by a man who began life as the son of a Maasai, and who read Shakespeare while tending cattle on his father's African farm. This boy then went to Rome to study art and architecture before moving to London to become a noted poet and writer. (What a CV!) He could only afford this tiny cottage in London's south, and to cover the damp he began carving elaborate fretwork using a tiny knife and timber found in skips. It took him 20 years, but he managed to cover the entire interior of the house with intricate fretwork inspired by Moorish architecture. Once he had finished, he died. It's a deeply moving space that's a shrine to creativity—and tenacity. It's difficult to see (each tour only allows six people and, not surprisingly, they're booked up months in advance), but well worth the effort. Put your name down for a tour. You'll remember this place long after you leave. (See also page 108.)

CHELSEA PHYSIC GARDEN This tranquil green space is often forgotten by both Londoners and tourists, although it's starting to gain popularity again. A walled space beside the Thames, it was established as the Apothecaries' Garden in London in 1673 for the purpose of training apprentices in identifying plants. The high walls around the garden create a warmer microclimate, allowing the survival of many non-native plants – such as the largest outdoor fruiting olive tree in Britain. The nearby river was also important as a transport route that linked the garden to other open spaces such as Putney Heath, facilitating easy movements of both plants and botanists. The name was eventually changed to 'physic' because a physic garden is a type of herb garden with medicinal plants, although the word 'physic' here refers to the science of healing. There are around 5000 edible, medicinal and other useful plants, including a 'dye plant' bed, and an area of scented flowers (including the rose-scented geranium). The garden and its labels encourage you to bend down and sniff or touch the plants (which everyone does), which contributes to the enjoyment. It's a wonderful place to wander on a sunny day (or even an overcast one!) learning about the secrets of plants and their many uses. Even nongardeners will appreciate the tranquility and gentle education. (See also page 92.)

EMERY WALKER TRUST This quiet tribute to artist, writer and designer William Morris is sometimes known by its formal name, the Emery Walker Trust and sometimes by its address, 7 Hammersmith Terrace. It's a tall Georgian house set right on the River Thames at Hammersmith that hides a beautiful secret—an Arts and Crafts interior that has been preserved exactly as it was in the lifetime of the printer Emery Walker (1851–1933), friend and mentor to William Morris, whose wallpapers, prints and fabrics can be found throughout. It is one of the last authentic Arts and Crafts interiors in Britain and certainly the most beautifully preserved. When Emery Walker and his family lived here, Hammersmith and Chiswick were popular not just because of the bucolic riverside location, but also because the area was home to many writers and artists. Other creative neighbours included the bookbinder TJ Cobden-Sanderson, with whom Walker set up the Doves Press in 1900, the calligrapher Edward Johnston, and the art critic FG Stephens. Walker's friend William Morris was a short distance away in Upper Mall, at a manor called Kelmscott House. Morris also used his own textiles, wallpapers and furniture in his own house, but much of these have been lost over the years, whereas Emery Walker and his family have retained theirs. It's a fascinating insight into not just William Morris' designs (they are *everywhere* in this house), but also the Arts and Crafts period and indeed life on the river in Chiswick at the end of the 19th century. (Note: This historic house will reopen for visitors in early 2017.) (See also page 110.)

GEFFRYE MUSEUM A little known museum in London's East End, the Geffrye is also known as the 'Museum of the Home'. It explores English houses from 1600 to the present day, focusing on the living rooms of London's influential and ever-changing middle and upper classes. It's set behind a grand garden but it also features it own large but charming garden at the rear, which is divided into garden designs of various periods in time: Victorian, Edwardian, and so on. It's difficult to know which is more interesting in this museum: the gardens or the interior design exhibitions? Both are surprisingly enlightening. The garden perhaps nudges ahead, if only because the various garden 'rooms' are such lovely spaces to be on a spring or summer day, learning about the exotics hothouses adored by the Victorians, the herb gardens favoured in the medieval era (the herb garden here is glorious), the modest gardens designed for Elizabethan townhouses and, of course, the Edwardian borders. The key is to read all the small signs and plaques, both outside and inside the museum; they're where the interesting bits are hidden. Even the small signs in the medieval herb garden are enthralling. (See also page 98.)

LEIGHTON HOUSE MUSEUM This is an astonishing historical property; a lavish, spectacular and spellbinding memorial to high Victorian taste. It's the former home and studio of the Victorian painter Frederic Leighton (1830–96), but it's not the kind of paint-splattered studio we usually associate with artists. No, this interior is as grand as any Moroccan palace, although it's perhaps more 'east' than 'west' in style. The highlight is the spectacular Arab Hall, an enormous, cathedral-sized entrance hall added in 1879 that's decorated with an intricate mosaic floor, a large (working) fountain, an extraordinary gold cupola, and walls and walls of blue and white Arabic tiles that were mostly saved from demolished mansions in Persia during Leighton's 'grand tours' of the Continent. It's astonishing. You barely even need to see the rest of the house to be amazed.

www.leightonhouse.co.uk

LONDON'S INDEPENDENT BOOKSHOPS London doesn't have the wealth of bookshops it once did (Jasper Conran once revealed he paid his way through university by buying and selling second-hand books to dealers), but there are still a great many bookish pleasures to be found. One of the loveliest is Heywood Hill in Mayfair, which is now owned by the Devonshires (of Chatsworth) who bought it to save it from closing. The Queen buys her books here. So, too, does Hugh Grant. (Although he does it under a friend's name to avoid people seeing what he likes to read. It's not certain whether the Queen does this, too. One wonders what her *nom de plume* would be.) There are always great titles on the front tables, but the real joy is to be had in the piles under the tables. There are often auctions of libraries from grand old estates too—usually found in the downstairs area, where many vintage editions are also kept. Potterton Books in Chelsea is another beautiful bookshop, and possibly the best bookshop in the world for second-hand design, architecture and gardening titles. It's small, but the stock is well curated, with a mix of vintage and new. The most interesting titles are displayed on the enormous display shelves to the right, or the bookshelves at the rear, where the priceless vintage gardening titles are kept.

LONDON'S MEWS (AND THEIR SECRET PUBS) The quaint term 'mews' is used to describe a row of stables, usually with carriage houses below and living quarters above, built around a paved yard or court. They were mostly found behind large city houses in inner London during the 17th and 18th centuries. Over the past decade, these mews dwellings have become highly desirable residences for their privacy, cute factor and (perhaps most of all) their precious garages—a rarity in London. However, they've also become havens for gardeners, who use the narrow lanes to create microclimates and tranquil urban streets scenes. In Kynance Mews, off Gloucester Road, many of the mews house owners have taken great efforts to create small or vertical gardens (look for the enormous wisteria trailing along the top of several of the cottages), and even the community bins have been installed in a huge planter box topped with flowers. In fact, Kynance Mews is one of London's best secret streets: step through its beautiful arches and you'll feel as though you're stepping into a storybook land. (Try and find the steps leading up to the church, and Launceston Place, another beautiful street.) Another lane, Stanhope Mews (near the Gloucester Road tube station in South Kensington), features houses fronted by brightly coloured flowers. Many of the mews in this prestigious area have featured in film sets and it's easy to see why; there's something romantic about these mews with their cobblestones and winding wisteria vines. Other cute mews include Spear Mews in Earl's Court, Bathurst Mews near Paddington Station, and Queen's Gate Mews off Gloucester Road, which has a great pub, the Queen's Arms pub at the end (30 Queens Gate Mews, Kensington). Indeed, there are several great pubs hidden away down mews lanes, although you often need a map to find them as they're sometimes elusive or well hidden, usually through an arch or down a local street that looks too private to have a pub at the end. The Horse and Groom and the Star Tavern in Belgravia are two charming pubs that are worth seeking out. The latter's appealing façade hides a mysterious past: apparently the Great Train Robbery was plotted upstairs. One can see how easy it might have been to be secretive here! (If you are looking for it, it's best to approach from Halkin Street to the north, as it's not easy to find.)

34

...cludes
... Vinci,
...nd
...s some
...st surviving
...and plants.

...ve far right:
...ard Knyff,
...w of Hampton
...OURCE
...t Indian,
...nd Garden
...OURCE

36 LONDON'S SECRET GARDENS Queen Mary's Rose Gardens of Regent's Park, the secret Sunken Garden of Kensington Gardens, the Rooftop Garden in Kensington, the Chelsea Physic Garden and St James's Park … London is dotted with secret gardens that are a sheer delight to discover and even lovelier to wander through. Perhaps the best is Queen Mary's Rose Garden, which has more than 12,000 roses, making it the largest rose garden in England. It's tricky to find, but follow the paths (and the rose bushes), and you'll inevitably stumble upon it. The prettiest part is the circular garden surrounded by rope arbours, where climbing roses and bushes bloom in June. Take a picnic or a packed lunch, or grab something to take away from the little café. On sunny days, it's a scented heaven. If you're in the east of London, try to see St Dunstan's, a church that was burnt down in the Great Fire, rebuilt, rebuilt again in the 18th century, and then destroyed in the Blitz by an incendiary bomb. Instead of being rebuilt for the third time, it was turned into a public garden, with the ivy and other foliage allowed to grow wild over the church's empty ruins and romantic window frames. It's quite, quite stunning and quite, quite haunting. The church itself is quietly beautiful, but the garden seems to grow happily in its own microclimate. There's even a banana palm and fig tree. In the south of London, meanwhile, there is the magnificent Victorian-era Horniman conservatory and the South London Botanical Institute, which offers an herbarium and even a fungi 'library'. (If you're serious about tracking down the city's secret green spaces, Abigail Willis' wonderful book *The London Garden Book A–Z* is a great guide.)

LONDON'S VICTORIAN LIDOS AND POOL (INCLUDING MARSHALL STREET BATHS) Most of us don't associate London with swimming, but in fact London has some refreshing, beautifully designed Victorian-era baths and lidos to wash away the jet lag and travel weariness. Just show up with your swimmers and a fiver, and dive on in. One of the most spectacular pools is the historic, listed, Victorian-era Marshall Street Baths off Regent Street in Soho, which is lined in white Sicilian marble. It was refurbished in 2010 after an injection of funds to save it from being lost to time and age, and is now just as elegant as it was when it was first created. In the summer, the outdoor lidos are also glorious swimming spots to spend an afternoon.

SIR JOHN SOANE'S APARTMENT One of the most complex, ambitious and exciting restoration projects in London in recent years, certainly for architecture and design fans, has been the private apartment of architect and collector Sir John Soane, situated above the Soane Museum. Having been closed to the public for 160 years, the space took more than a decade to restore before finally opening in May 2015. This top-floor apartment is where Soane and his wife lived and slept, and includes Mrs Soane's morning room, a bathroom, a lavish bedroom, an Oratory and a quirky book passage. However, the most spectacular part is the Model Room, which displays 40 of the finest architectural models in Soane's collection, many on an unusual three-tiered model stand that dominates the room. There are also priceless paintings, including a beautiful study by Turner, plus drawings, watercolours and stained glass. The museum downstairs is also extraordinary. There are more than 20,000 architectural drawings and antiquities here, all displayed in a mix of conventional hangings and hidden cabinets and secrets panels. The most ingenious of these spaces is a moving wall that can display different artworks (Canaletto, Turner, Hogarth) at different times. Soane's library is breathtaking; the breakfast room has a beautiful domed ceiling, while the magnificent Monument Court in the lower floor contains an Egyptian sarcophagus of alabaster, so fine that it's almost translucent, that was carved for the pharaoh Seti I (1291–1278 BC) and discovered in his tomb in Egypt's Valley of the Kings. The *Oxford Dictionary of Architecture* calls the museum "one of the most complex, intricate, and ingenious series of interiors ever conceived." It is delightful, enlightening, educational and, best of all, utterly surprising. To preserve all the delicate pieces, only 70 visitors are allowed at a time, which often means a queue outside. And it's become even worse since the museum became something of a must-see destination. (It attracted 110,000 visitors in 2015.) But be patient: it's worth the wait!

THE STORED ARCHIVES OF THE V&A If you like fashion, try and get a tour to Blythe House in West Kensington, which is where the V&A keeps all its archives and collections that aren't on show in the galleries of the museum on Cromwell Road. There are more the 100,000 items of vintage Chanel, Schiaparelli, Balenciaga, Dior and more. It is an extraordinary place. The vast textiles collection also includes lace, embroidery, antique linen, tapestries and wall-hangings, while hats, shoes and fans are kept in a separate section of the same building. Members of the public can join one of the monthly tours, or visit to research textiles for their own fashion or interiors projects. Entrance to the centre is by appointment only and tours run on the last Friday morning of each month (lasting 45 minutes). It's free to attend, but booking is essential. Email clothworkers@vam.ac.uk to reserve a place. *Note: The venue for the Clothworkers' Centre may be changing in early 2017; see www.vam.ac.uk for updates.*

THE FABRIC STORES OF KINGS ROAD, FULHAM ROAD AND BEYOND Many people adore fabric stores, and London offers an incredible array of them, although sadly not as many now as years ago. They are part of Britain's rich history in the textile trade, and stock everything from flamboyant embroideries to sumptuous silks, linens and wools. The most concentrated clusters are along Fulham Road and the lower end of King's Road, home to the vast Chelsea Harbour Design Centre, a veritable who's who of textiles, from Tissus d'Hélène (a wonderful jumble of beautiful tactile fabrics) to Brunschwig & Fils, Kravet, GP and J Baker and Samuel and Sons. There are more than one hundred fabric houses here, so leave a few hours. Some are trade-only, but you can ask for samples of your preferred fabrics. If you want to get around the trade-only restrictions, try Designers Guild on King's Road, which stocks Ralph Lauren, William Yeoward, Christian Lacroix and others, as well as Designers Guild's own collections (there is another DG store on Marylebone High Street), and Colefax and Fowler on Fulham Road, where you can buy exquisite fabrics from the likes of French house Manuel Canovas. Neither store requires an interior designer's trade card; they're some of the few places you can buy Manuel Canovas, Ralph Lauren and Designers Guild fabrics this way.

THE NATIONAL PORTRAIT GALLERY AND ITS RESTAURANT A little-known London secret is the top floor of the National Portrait Gallery, which has enormous windows that look right over Trafalgar Square, Big Ben and the rooftops of London. Lovely for a drink or dinner at twilight in the summer, looking out onto all the London icons. And of course the portraits in the galleries below are fairly amazing, too.

This page from top to bottom A shopfront in Notting Hill and a textile design from William Morris, seen at his former home in Chiswick

THE RIVERSIDE PATHS, PUBS AND HOMES OF CHISWICK This part of London is almost rural in its setting: close your eyes and you could be forgiven for thinking you were in deepest Oxfordshire. Lined with a mix of grand 17th- and 18th-century houses and sweet cottages with charming gardens, it makes for a lovely walk on a sunny day. Try to time your itinerary so you finish at the wonderfully evocative old riverside pub called the Dove, which has a *Guinness Book of Records* entry for the smallest bar in the world. (Don't worry; you don't need to squeeze in there; there's another larger, orangery-style bar in the same pub that overlooks the river.) Grab a drink and watch the rowers racing down the Thames. When you've finished, head to Chiswick High Road for dozens of beautiful boutiques and restaurants. Don't miss the Old Cinema for antiques and High Road House hotel for a drink. As an urban village, it's one of London's best-kept secrets. No wonder Colin Firth and others have bought homes here. It's a pocket of pure bliss.

There are many more design, architecture, garden and decorating secrets in the pages to follow! Read on to find out more about these and many other destinations.

Right *The riverside path that winds through Chiswick village*
Following pages *The sublime Wild at Heart florist, which operates out of the whimsical architectural folly called 'Turquoise Island' in Notting Hill* **(left);** *A front door painted a perfect shade of Tiffany Blue* **(right)**

HOTELS AND

DINING

44

Clockwise from top left *The charming Wedgewood-blue entrance of The Cranley; treats at The Ambersand; a terrace room at Number Sixteen; quirky cricket ball door handles at Dorset Square; the boldly decorated parlour at the Ambersand* **Opposite** *The red, black and white palette of this suite at Blakes reflects the colours of London's famous black cabs, white architecture and red telephone boxes*

HOTELS FOR FASHION, ARCHITECTURE, DECORATING AND DESIGN FANS

Once upon a time, London hotels were terribly old-fashioned affairs. Dear old doormen would shuffle to your black cab, assist you to the street and then carry your bags, their old shoulders slumping under the strain of all those shoes and clothes you'd packed for the unpredictable English weather, to the charming reception. Your booking would then be found, stern housemaids would have to be asked whether the room was ready, and multi-tasking concierges would dash to and fro through the foyer, arms and legs awry like an octopus, sorting out guest requests. In the corner, meanwhile, there was usually a bespectacled old guest settled into a velvet wingback armchair, wrist firmly gripping an overflowing G&T, who always lifted his head in convivial greeting. Well, fortunately—or unfortunately—this is no more. Today's hotels are sleek operations staffed by hipsters with finely cut beards and girls who look like they went to top schools. The guests' luggage is often Rimowa carry-ons or Milanese-made leather weekenders. And the services for guests often extend from helicopters to event planners. Nothing is too much trouble. When one American VIP guest at a Knightsbridge hotel wanted her suite to look "like an English conservatory", the staff happily dragged in half a country garden.

But with all this modern design and modern service comes an old-fashioned dilemma: which hotel do you choose? Do you go with the all-white, Japanese-style design where minimalism and decluttering has been elevated to a fine art? Do you go with the multi-coloured, beautiful, textured hotel, featuring the latest fabrics from global designers, that is so eye-catching it's already been featured in *World of Interiors* or *Cabana* magazines? Do you go with the fashionable new bolthole, where Bill Clinton and David Cameron have already dined and departed? Or … do you opt for the under-the-radar design cutie, a place so off the media grid that not even the super-savvy globe-trotting crowd knows about it, where staff remember your name and your favourite drink, and chocolate is waiting in your room upon check-in, and the library is stocked with gorgeous design, fashion and architecture books just waiting to be perused. Hotels can have antiques, art and everything in between sourced from far and wide, and they often detail the suppliers, and also the fabrics and textiles used throughout, in framed mood boards, just in case you want to seek them out for yourself. All of which makes choosing one difficult to decide. Well, here are a few beautiful rooms to help you.

TIPS FOR FINDING YOUR IDEAL HOTEL

As with any city, the best way to decide on a hotel is to work out which neighbourhood you want to spend the most time in. Some people target a hotel based on its 'hot factor' (or at the other end of the decision scale, its cheap prices), but choosing hotels based on these things doesn't always equate to a good time. Indeed, it can leave you feeling as though you've spent too much money for The Cool Factor, and not really gained much by the experience either.

Far better to find a hotel close to the things you love. Then you can wander your chosen neighbourhood at leisure. Believe it or not, this will make a lot of difference to your stay. When you can easily walk to the things you want to see and do, it cuts down on not only transport time but also the costs of tubes or taxis.

So, for example, if you're a theatre, shopping and restaurant nut who wants constant stimulation and nightlife, you're best off being based in the West End. If you're someone who prefers greenery and a walk or run through a park in the morning or at night, then consider basing yourself in Kensington or South Kensington, close to Hyde Park and Kensington Gardens, and all the green spaces of these neighbourhoods. Do you want to hit the shops? Look for a hotel in Chelsea, Brompton Cross, Knightsbridge, Notting Hill or Marylebone. Do you prefer antiques, independent boutiques and textile stores? Pimlico, Fulham Road and the south end of King's Road are your best bet. And if you want to be surrounded by history, great old architecture, and classic pubs alongside glamorous or unique new stores and restaurants, try Bloomsbury, the East End, Chiswick, or Mayfair.

SAVING MONEY ON YOUR HOTEL BILL

Studies conducted by online sites, such as Trivago.com and other hotel-booking companies have found that the best hotel deals are found a month or two in advance. Book any earlier and you're not likely to save any money; any later and you may have to pay more. The reason why? Hotels want to fill their rooms in advance but they want to make money, too. The closer you get to your stay, the more likely it is that rooms are full, and hence you'll pay a premium for the last ones available. However, if you book a month or two before your stay, the hotel will have most likely filled half and will be looking to fill the rest quickly, so its books look healthy going forward. Some hotels even do 'snap' sales around this time, to fill the vacant rooms. (Hotels are usually at their most expensive three or more months in advance.)

If you really want to save money on your hotel bill—or even stay in an expensive hotel for a cheap rate—try booking a Saturday or Sunday night. That's when many city hotels drop their prices by up to one-third, as the cashed-up business crowd has left London and hotels want to fill their rooms. You can sometimes find rooms at five-star hotels for less than £100 a night. Sunday nights are always cheap, as the weekend revellers have left and gone back to the country, and hotels are looking to fill rooms before the business travellers move in on Mondays.

If you're keen on upgrades, check in as late as possible. There is more chance that the hotel will have run out of standard rooms and will give you a higher room category. (Oh, and it helps to be pleasant to the people at the reception desk!)

For great hotel deals, look for snap sales on booking sites such as TableHotels.com or Booking.com. (These are the preferred booking sites for many business travellers. Other sites aren't quite as professional, and don't allow easy cancellations.) Both TabletHotels.com and Booking.com often offer spontaneous sales or discounts on certain hotels or cities (you need to be a subscriber to Tablet, but it's free). These snap sales are fast, but if you're quick you can pick up some great bargains. You can even find five-star London hotels for one-quarter their standard rate. The time of year is also a factor in finding great prices. If you want a really low-price London stay, try the off-peak months of late November to early December, and early January through to February / March / April. Late November / early December is a particularly fantastic time to visit London because the Christmas lights and festivities are in full swing, yet the hotel rates are the lowest of the year.

Finally, if you're travelling solo, ask for a single room: these are even cheaper than the usual double rooms and suites, and the beds in many hotels are three-quarter size, which are fine for one person. But if you're claustrophobic, check the size of the room! Some are squishier than others. But you can get lucky, too. The single rooms in the Dorset Square Hotel and Number Sixteen are beautiful, with enormous windows, magnificent fabrics and stunning modern bathrooms.

BEST HOTELS FOR THE DESIGN AND GLAMOUR CROWDS

AMBERSAND A stylish and relatively new arrival on London's hotel scene, the wonderfully named Ambersand is a clever segueway between the classic, comfortable British hotel and the sleek, new, modern style of design. The first thing that tells you it's a little different is the fabulous interior design. The entrance is elegant but fun (staff wear jeans), while the drawing room is a sweep of Wedgewood blue and British-telephone-box red, with colour-coordinated afternoon tea to match (a table full of courtesy cakes and pasties). Corners feature curiosities and objets d'art, while the corridors are themed to botany, music, ornithology and astronomy in tribute to the nearby museums. It's British and yet not British, witty and whimsical yet not too-over-the-top, and completely, utterly delightful. The best rooms are the large ones, with velvet headboards, high ceilings, and luxurious swathes of curtains, but even the smaller ones are studies in sophistication. Perhaps the only thing to note is the slight rumble of trains (the hotel is situated over the tube line), but things like the well-stocked bookshelves, the cheery staff, the free Wi-Fi and the complimentary soft drinks from the minibar more than make up for the small annoyances.

10 Harrington Road, South Kensington, London. www.ampersandhotel.com

BLAKES Opened in 1978, Blakes was one of the first (some say the first) pioneering boutique hotels in the world that really took interior design and pushed the boundaries out well past the places that hotels had ever gone. Designed by the beautiful and talented Australian designer Anouska Hempel (once a Bond girl), it was designed to be an ode to the glamour of travel. Each suite was decorated to a theme—Empire, Africa, Biedermeier, Corfu—and filled with vintage Louis Vuitton trunks or striped fabrics that were reminiscent of a Marrakech tent in the desert. The foyer, meanwhile, was a poetic paean to the Grand Tour, with more vintage Louis Vuitton trunks, a wicker-covered staircase, books on travel, fashion, glamour, art and other exotic topics, and birdcages and other colonial antiques from places deep in South-East Asia. Wherever you looked in Blakes, there was something to surprise, beguile and delight. Anouska Hempel's eye for proportion and design was everywhere. Not surprisingly, it was a hit with celebrities, particularly the rock and model kind. (Guests have also included Karl Lagerfeld, Valentino and Ralph Lauren, who was no doubt inspired by it all.) Then came the decade of minimalism and decluttering, and hotels pared back their interiors to barely nothing (which also saved on design). Blakes, some critics said, looked like a relic from the 1980s. It felt like a Merchant Ivory film that had faded with time. But then came a revival. The hotel was sold and the new owners brought Anouska Hempel back to work her magic. Spaces were refreshed and rooms revived, although some of the classic elements, such as the upholstered walls, were retained. Today, it has that lovely, lived-in feel so reminiscent of English country houses. Yes, there are some slightly worn corners of the upholstered walls, but they only add to the English charm. Overall, the recent facelift has elevated it to 'fabulous' once again. The best rooms are the Director's Doubles (Sunday nights are cheapest), but if you can afford it, go for the grand Library Suite. Staff are lovely; nothing is too much trouble here, and they don't care whether you're Lady Gaga (who stays here) or someone on a business trip. Everyone is treated with genuine care. It's a fantasy of a place that sentimentalists and romantics will adore. A place that reminds us that, beneath the jet lag and weariness of it all, travel is still truly wonderful.

33 Roland Gardens, South Kensington, London. www.blakeshotel.com

COVENT GARDEN HOTEL No list of beautiful London hotels would be complete without one or even several of the properties of the Firmdale Group. Founded by Kit Kemp and her husband Tim, the group has just opened its ninth property, Ham Yard. However, it's their Covent Garden Hotel that is still one of the prettiest in the Firmdale Set. It's here that you'll see all the vibrant, colourful, whimsical and quintessentially British textiles that have come to define the brand and distinguish the Kemps' hotels from all the rest. It's where the textiles dance and play as if at a summer party; behold pinks and canary yellows and crimsons and every shade in between. The best room—perhaps the most beautiful room in all of London—is the garden- and fashion-themed Loft Suite (Room 303 / 304), which is so elegant that Armani's fashion entourage often stay here when they're in town. There are dressmakers' mannequins, watering cans, horticultural prints and lush fabrics throughout. It's a fantasy of textiles and design, just like the whole hotel.

10 Monmouth Street, Covent Garden, London, WC2. www.firmdalehotels.com

DEAN STREET TOWNHOUSE The Dean Street Townhouse is adored, it seems, by half of London. The downstairs restaurant that spills out into the narrow street is certainly a *tableau vivant* of laughing, chattering, gossiping, drinking and flirting between beautiful people. The hotel is right in the heart of all the West End action, and so close to the bars of Soho that you can fall out of a dry bed and straight into a wet martini, but why would you go anywhere else when there's clearly so much action going on right here? And yet it's also a very discreet place. People like Jude Law and Gwyneth Paltrow come and go without being papped by pesky photographers zeroing in on their bottoms. Part of the reason for this is that the hotel is hidden behind a dignified, quiet façade, which—it has to be said—encourages illicit liaisons and clandestine meetings! Rooms can be on the tight side—the smallest are teeny, two-store affairs where the bedroom is reached by a circular staircase to a mezzanine—but the compensation is gorgeous colours, sumptuous textiles, amazing antiques, luxurious bathrooms and the Soho Group's famous Cowshed beauty products (guaranteed to wash the jet lag away). The larger suites are, of course, better, and feature free-standing claw-tub baths, but don't feel you need spend your money unless you're a couple or used to unadulterated luxury. The sweet singles are just fine for business travellers and those flying solo. Instead, save your pounds for the famous restaurant downstairs, where you're liable to see a few familiar faces in the crowd: it's a fave of TV personalities, music industry peeps, and other Soho-loving souls. The only downside is that the hotel is part of the Soho House Group, so rates for nonmembers are more expensive than for members, but don't let that deter you. In fact, all of Soho House's properties are gorgeous, so join up for the discount.

69–71 Dean Street, Soho, London. www.deanstreettownhouse.com

DORSET SQUARE Although it's a little out of the way, this is a truly enchanting hideaway created by Kit Kemp of the famous Firmdale Group. Quirky botanical wallpaper, cricket-bat still lifes (inspired by the nearby Lords Cricket Ground), a boldly decorated parlour and restaurant, and pretty rooms with luxurious fabrics (a signature of Ms Kemp) mean it's a firm favourite with the design crowd. The sophisticated stores of Marylebone High Street and the famous roses of Queen Anne's garden in Regent's Park are a short walk away. A real London secret.

39–40 Dorset Square, Marylebone, London. www.firmdalehotels.com

DUKES Not many travellers know about the Edwardian beauty of Dukes, because it's discreet—almost too discreet for its own good. This is not the Chiltern Firehouse. There are no celebs being papped as they stumble out the door. No, this is possibly London's most unobtrusive hotel, which is why it's long being the haunt of dukes and other members of the aristocracy. Authors, too. Ian Fleming loved staying here. He not only found inspiration for the line "shaken, not stirred" while having a drink here, he also named his hero, James Bond, after St James's and Bond Streets. Everything here is the epitome of British class. There's even a Cognac and Cigar Courtyard Garden for the gentlemen, and a pistachio-green and hot-pink Champagne Lounge for the ladies. The best thing about it is, if you'd like a picnic, your butler will prepare blankets, hot-water bottles, booze and a hamper full of high-end treats and then set the whole lot up in Green Park for you. Could hotel service get any better than that?

35 St James's Place, Mayfair, London. www.dukeshotel.com

FLEMINGS Few people know about this Mayfair hideaway, but after the glam refurbishment it's just been through, that's sure to change. The style media will be all over this honey. The knockout here is not the location—although Mayfair is now one of the coolest places to shop or strutt, with an influx of new and great fashion boutiques and bars. Instead, the drawcard is the public area, which includes a coolly elegant drawing room decorated in jewel shades of emerald with an Indian mural painted in panels on the wall, and a cosy bar with a fireplace, peacock-coloured velvet banquettes, fashion and design books to flick through, and touches of dazzling yellow (the 'in' shade in decorating). If you can afford it, opt for the suite that opens onto a private garden; one of the few hotel rooms in London with one.

7–12 Half Moon Street, Mayfair, London. www.flemings-mayfair.co.uk

50 **NUMBER SIXTEEN** Named after its address in a leafy street of South Kensington, Number Sixteen is one of the sweetest hotels in London. It's the darling of the Firmdale Hotel group, which was founded by Kit and Tim Kemp and which continues to produce some of the most beautiful, most talked-about hotels in town. Their newest offering, Ham Yard, dominated the headlines of newspaper travel supplements in 2015, yet it's this little hideaway in South Ken that continues to lure guests. It's actually a collection of stuccoed townhouses, whose crisp white exterior belies the vibrant colour palettes inside. Kit Kemp has become famous for her use of pinks, greens and reds, and Number Sixteen is a swirl of all three; a real aesthete's delight. The parlour and library are painterly scenes of fabric, artwork, books and colour, while the cute glass-encased conservatory overlooking the large garden (rare in London hotels) is enchanting for breakfast and afternoon tea. Rooms are similarly sublime, especially if you can afford to upgrade to the larger queen rooms and suites. But even the single rooms are special, especially if you land one of the ones at the front, which have French doors leading out to a huge, sunny terrace overlooking the street. They may be petite in size, but they make up for it in personality, with Schiaparelli-pink walls, theatrical drapes, pretty desks, and pristine white marble bathrooms. No wonder people love this place. It's everything you hope to find in a boutique hotel; a real home away from home that looks like a *Vogue Living* spread, but welcomes guests like a much-loved aunt!

16 Sumner Place, South Kensington, London. www.firmdalehotels.com

THE PELHAM The Pelham is tailor-made for design lovers. It was one of hotel designer Kit Kemp's first experiments (athough it's since been sold to new owners) and it still reflects her skilful touch. Luxury textiles are given priority here, to the point where several suites have framed 'mood boards' of fabric swatches outside the doors showing the textiles and fabric houses that were used. (I told you it was a design-lover's kind of place.) The foyer is one of the most beautiful hotel spaces in London: a combination of pale, stripped-back floorboards, olive-green walls and a carved ebony-black reception desk: a delightfully English triptych of black, white and green. The front drawing room (which looks and feels as comfy as a proper drawing room) is an equally understated space of mushroom and grey shades, as is the subdued chocolate and red library at the rear; both have cosy fireplaces, honesty bars and an atmosphere that makes you want to settle in and never leave. But it's the rooms where the design really comes alive. Each is decorated in an individual way; one may be fitted with pretty cream and raspberry pink; another in rich, romantic aubergine and mauve shades. Fabrics are key and the patterns are surprising; it's a rare thing to find a window drape matching a bedspread.

Many guests have their own favourites. Downstairs, there's a stunning turquoise and tomato-red restaurant (used as a breakfast room), where nonguests can enjoy the hotel's charm. Everything about the Pelham is a little quirky, a little eccentric, but it's all done in a delightful way—as only the English can do. If you're into interior design, textiles and decoration, you'll love it here.

15 Cromwell Place, South Kensington, London. www.pelhamhotel.co.uk

W LONDON LEICESTER SQUARE Some people love or loath W Hotels. They were very 'in' for a while, and like anything that's publicised too much, they then went 'out'. You could argue that they were over-branded. But they still have their fans. Indeed, the London W has many of them. And it's easy to see why. The hotel is set within a startling white-glass building on Leicester Square that's very un-London, and gives you a taste of the shimmering design to be found beyond. Inside, hundreds of mirrored disco balls dangle from the ceilings, right from the lobby through the hallways, making you feel ever-so-slightly like you're John Travolta in *Stayin' Alive*. Everything seems very energetic and enthusiastic; even the rooms are categorised as 'Wonderful', 'Spectacular', or 'Fabulous'. And although they're merely sleeping spaces (let's refrain from adding anything dirty here), they're firmly designed for the party crowd, with specially lit makeup mirrors, white-leather salon chairs, Bliss cosmetics, art and design books, and of course the requisite up-lit bars with lots of martini glasses. So you can start your night early. The 'hot spots' in the hotel are the Spice Market restaurant (bad pun), which comes alive after midnight, and a VIP bar called Wyld, with a disco ball. If you feel too old for it all, you probably are.

10 Wardour Street, Leicester Square, London.
www.wlondon.co.uk or www.whotels.com

Opposite *The black-and-white shades of a suite at the Soho Hotel*

52

BEST HOTELS FOR BUSINESS

ECCLESTON SQUARE HOTEL For many years, the neighbourhoods of Belgravia and Pimlico suffered from being squished awkwardly between the chic shopping strips of Chelsea and the commuter traffic of Victoria Station. But then came a revival for this forgotten village, and now Pimlico is one of the prettiest parts of SW London. Along with the influx of new design stores and gorgeous bistros, there are several lovely new hotels and pubs. The Eccleston Square Hotel is one. Tailor-made for the fashion and style crowd travelling for business or trade shows, it's been formed from a beautiful old Grade II–listed Georgian building, and the new interior is just as understated as the old architecture. A monochromatic palette prevails, so it's perfect for those who like wearing black, black and more black, although the rooms are decked out in rich hues of chocolate, marle grey and the particular shade of beige-camel that many expensive cashmere shawls come in. But behind the calm luxe lies a whole lot of complex technology. The hotel has been wired for high-tech guests and features all sorts of electronic wizardry. Every room not only comes with a super-sprung Hästen bed, known as the most comfortable (and expensive) beds in the world (Angelina Jolie has one), but also an iPad2 that can fine-tune the room lighting, curtains, music and sound and the large 3D, flat-screen TV. The luxury marble bathrooms, meanwhile, include a hidden TV in the bathroom mirror, massage showers and a 'smart glass' wall that turns opaque instantly at the touch of a button. Even the jaded business travellers will be impressed.

37 Eccleston Square, Belgravia, London, www.ecclestonsquarehotel.com

THE GORE The Gore is a London institution, but strangely it doesn't seem to register on the radar of travel writers and journalists as much as the 'hip hotels'. That doesn't really matter. In fact, it's far better because the rates stay low and you can always get a room. And you can bet that its loyal fans still book in, year after year. The hotel is located near the Royal Albert Hall, so it's great if you're in town for a concert (even those not staying like to use its bar for a drink before shows). It's also a few steps from Hyde Park so its location is ideal for those who like a run through the park. Inside, the interior sits on the traditional side, but it's done with bold colour and inspiring design elements. There is a beautiful library full of books, with daily newspapers and free coffee, tea and cakes, a gorgeous restaurant, and the aforementioned lively bar. But the most uplifting parts of this place are the rooms. The larger ones recall grand rooms in a country house, with four-poster beds, period paintings and lavish furnishing. The smaller ones are no less impressive. Everything about The Gore is dignified and endearing. The staff even remember your name whenever you walk in the front door. A true London classic. Let's hope it never changes.

190 Queen's Gate, South Kensington, London, www.gorehotel.com

This page from left to right *A suite at The Pelham; the garden at Number Sixteen*
Opposite from left to right *A guest's private balcony at Blakes; detail at the Soho Hotel*

"Hotel design is what makes a space intriguing beyond being just lovely to look at—it draws you in, captivates your imagination."

—Hotel designer Kit Kemp, co-founder of Firmdale Hotels

BEST HOTELS FOR HISTORY FANS

54 **CORINTHIA HOTEL** Formerly the historic Metropole Hotel where MI9 and the Special Operations Executive were based during World War II, the newly restored Corinthia features the kind of coolly glamorous interiors for which London is becoming renowned. You know, the kind that David Collins made famous before he sadly passed away, leaving a great void to fill. In fact, David Collins' Design Studio designed Corinthia's beautiful blue Art Deco–inspired Massimo bistro, which won Best New Design in *Time Out* magazine's 2011 awards. But it's not just the bar that has everyone wishing David Collins' Studio would do their own home. Everything about the Corinthia is sleek and stunning and speaks of money, from the guests (think: Middle Eastern entourages) to the floral displays. (There's even an in-house florist, Ercole Moroni, should you want daily posies for your suite.) Approximately half a billion dollars were spent on the interiors alone, which feature a Baccarat chandelier, and a bar with a 6-metre-long (20-foot-long) piano off which people sip cocktails laced with violet liqueur. (The violets are probably even grown on the rooftop, such is the attention to detail here.) Harrods has an outpost on-site, too, just in case you need some new garb to go out in. It's a grand hotel in every way. But it's not gauche, as some wealthy Americans might say. In fact, it's arguably one of the most elegant city hotels in the world. But there's a catch: it's expensive. If you have to ask, you can't afford it. Go for a drink and admire it from afar. Or splurge and book the curved-walled River Suite, with its sophisticated blue hues and views of the River Thames. You'll remember it forever.

Whitehall Place, London. www.corinthia.com/hotels/london

HAZLITT'S Hazlitt's is the former home of English writer and poet William Hazlitt, who tragically died in poverty in 1830 but left a magnificent legacy, in both words and the design of this extraordinary Soho hideaway. Hazlitt actually died in one of three adjoining townhouses that form the hotel, but don't let that put you off, because the place is more of a celebration of his spirit and creativity. The hotel has become a haven for literary types who love the mood (dark and cosy), the character (slightly eccentric, with sloping floorboards and period portraits), and the interior design (a theatrical mix of antiques, busts, classical statues, French beds, free-standing bath-tubs, secret loos and gilt dressing tables). The most popular room is the suite with a sitting room, a working fireplace (rare for London hotels), a bath filled from the beak of a life-sized bronze eagle, and a private rooftop terrace with a retractable glass roof. It's utterly seductive, and particularly popular with romantics and creative types, and also—not surprisingly—authors, who traditionally leave signed copies of their works when they depart. Hazlitt would be pleased. Then again, he may not have appreciated the competition.

6 Frith Street, Soho, London. www.hazlittshotel.com

ST PANCRAS RENAISSANCE It's a clever idea, to create a hotel in a train station where the busy Eurostar departs and arrives. (Those 6am departures to Paris are a nightmare when the first tube trains barely start at the same time.) But this is no long-forgotten place tarted up for business commuters dashing off to France for the day. It's a gorgeously grand, stupendously beautiful, high-Victorian-Gothic folly of a place. It's the hotel version of Downton Abbey. Or the Orient Express. Or any of the other over-the-top interiors we've romanticised over the years. The building originally opened in 1873 and was, at the height of its glory, the greatest Victorian building in London. Then, from the Depression until the 1960s, it fell onto bad times. It took 40 years for the restoration to be finished, but the result is as splendid as the Mark I version. The towers and turrets are still there, as well as the Gothic architectural features (some rooms have 5.5-metre (18-foot) ceilings and huge Gothic windows), but the dark, gloomy, locked-up rooms of the past decades have gone. Now there are sumptuous, richly decorated interiors, with lovely wallpaper, thick carpets, even delightful stencil work. If you love architecture, opt for one of the 38 quirkier rooms, particularly those with a view of the glass-ceilinged train station. If you can afford it, ask for the Royal Suite: housed in the former Venetian Ballroom, it's a 279-square-metre (3000-square-foot) study in luxury with walk-in wardrobes, a drawing room (a drawing room!), a study and a dining table that serves 20. Just in case you happen to have a few guests. If you can't afford the rate for the rooms (honestly, it might be cheaper just to go to Paris!), slip in for a drink before your train departs: the former ticketing office has been converted into a magnificent bar and restaurant. A lot of insiders say this place is favoured by those who are having an affair. See if you can spot them! (Clearly, they can't afford to take their clandestine meeting all the way to the Left Bank …)

Euston Road, Kings Cross, London. www.marriott.com.au

THE CONNAUGHT HOTEL If you've ever walked into a Ralph Lauren store and admired the interior design and fittings, well, the Connaught is the inspiration. Mr Lauren stayed here for one year and was so impressed by the magnificent mahogany staircase climbing five stories to a domed skylight, he copied it for his flagship store in New York. The Connaught and Sutherland Suites are a study in English elegance, with interiors and furniture done in an Adam-style palette of pale pinks, eau-de-Nil and Wedgwood blues. But the prize for the best room in the hotel, possibly in the whole of Mayfair, is a tie between Oliver's Terrace Suit, which features its own rooftop garden designed by Chelsea winner Tom Stuart-Smith, and David Collins' apartment, which resembles a beautiful beach house.

Carlos Place, Mayfair, London. www.the-connaught.co.uk

TOWN HALL Bethnal Green often creates a question mark in the minds of those who don't know London that well. Is it near Spitalfields? Clerkenwell? Well, it's actually a single stop past Liverpool Street. And it's very, very cool. Ironically, the area was once synonymous with gangsters and other dangerous dudes, but since it's been cleaned up it's gathered a whole legion of fans. They flock to this 'hood to drink, dine and shop at eccentric, bohemian little boutiques. And so the Town Hall Hotel opened to cater to this cool new crowd (as well as the rest of us who are following in their wake). The building was formerly a monstrous government structure with gorgeous architecture but little internal soul. The owners spent a fortune saving the façade and then refashioning the interior, which has been dubbed 'subtle but expensive Deco style'. There's a lot of Australian walnut, polished mahogany and white marble, but there's also a lot of quirky vintage stuff too, which harks back to the building's origins as a government office. It's all been done with great flair, and in fact is slightly reminiscent of Paul Smith. There's even a vending machine from the 1930s. And recently there was a pop-shop for a florist that featured a cucumber water fountain. As well, there's a very good restaurant, which won a Michelin star. However, the rooms are where the value is. Every room has a kitchen, so you could settle in for a week, or four. It's all so clever that the hotel won the prestigious RICS London award for Building Conservation, as well as the national Project of the Year Award.

Patriot Square, Bethnal Green, London.

www.townhallhotel.com

Right *Hazlitt's hotel in Soho*

CHILTERN FIREHOUSE Ah, the Chiltern. What can be said that hasn't already been uttered in the countless column inches written about it in international newspapers and magazines? This former firehouse in Marylebone has been a 'hot spot' (forgive the pun) since owner Andre Balaz, the suave hotelier behind Hollywood's Chateau Marmont and the Mercer in New York, opened it in 2015. Clinton's been. So has David Cameron. And Kate Moss and David Beckham and half of Hollywood. For a while there you couldn't get in, it seemed, unless you had an Oscar or BAFTA poking out of your handbag / manbag. But now the fuss has been hosed down, and the Chiltern's garden courtyard is easier to get in for an afternoon drink or dinner. Or you can opt for the gorgeous gold-and-mustard-hued bar, a country-style retreat in the middle of Marylebone. The hotel is pretty too, with the same tasteful blue and yellow hues and piles of velvety chairs to sink into. The spacious rooms come with marble vanity tables, pewter baths and access to a personal concierge. On the bedside table sits a telephone and a card with a simple message: 'Dial 0 for anything.' Go for the people-watching or just go for the award-winning food; whatever you go for, the Chiltern still has one of the best moods in London.

1 Chiltern Street, Marleybone, London.
www.chilternfirehouse.com

58

Opposite *The parlour of The Pelham in South Kensington*
This page top to bottom *The sophistication of Number Sixteen; Dorset Square*

INTRIGING NEWBIES

BATTY LANGLEY'S Batty Langley was an eccentric English garden and architectural designer (1696–1751) and prolific writer who produced a number of pattern books and designs for early-18th-century architects and joiners, mostly for 'Gothick' structures such as houses, summerhouses, garden buildings and curious things such as *cabinets de verdure*. His books and writings were often derided by other designers, who saw them as a bit of cockscombry. (Horace Walpole, whose Gothick villa, Strawberry Hill, at Twickenham in London is still open to visitors, despised him.) George Washington, however, adored him, and used many of his design principles at Mount Vernon in the United States, as did many English estate owners. His eccentricity was most evident in his childrens' names—Hiram, Euclid, Vitruvius and Archimedes. So why is all this relevant? Well, for centuries this man has remained something of an enigma, but now his name is coming to light largely through the efforts of two self-confessed 'daft old gits' with a penchant for the 'batty'. Pun intended. Hoteliers Douglas Blain and Peter McKay—former journalists, travel operators and antiques collectors—had already made their mark in the hotel game with the marvellously charismatic and still-successful hotels Hazlitt's in Soho and the Rookery in Clerkenwell. They were also founding members of the Spitalfields Trust, which saves and restores old houses. But they weren't content, and so they created this, their best project yet. 'Atmosphere' is the name of the game here, according to the two gentlemen, and there is so much of it you might think you're in a BBC period drama. Furnished in every shade of crimson, rose, chilli, pink and claret, the hotel also features pops of mustard yellow, olive green and an elegant mid-hue blue. But it's the crimson you remember. It's the crimson that makes Batty so beautiful. Like the two sister hotels, this feels like a private residence. Or a club. The front door is locked unless you are staying, and there is no sign outside. There is also no restaurant. Breakfast in bed is supplied instead. Just like in a private home. The welcoming parlour contains antique furnishings, handwoven rugs, a working fireplace, and panelled walls. Most of the rooms have 17th- or 18th-century beds, which are rather lush and indulgent and definitely assist the sleep factor, while many have mahogany Carlton House desks with secret drawers and compartments (just try finding them). Many of the guest bathrooms contain cast-iron bath-tubs, period fittings and restored vintage showers. The best suite is the one with a marble bath the size of a sarcophagus, which was flown in from Tuscany and installed by crane when the roof was off. (Other rooms don't miss out on bathroom luxuries; many feature beautiful swan-head bath taps and brass fittings.) But there is technology, too. Such as TV sets concealed in folding mirrors. But the main thing here is atmosphere. Lots and lots of it. In fact, when the duo refurbished the hotel they realised the squeaks had gone from the floorboards and asked the builders to put them back in. How's that for authenticity?

12 Folgate Street, Spitalfields, London. www.battylangleys.com

> *"All good hotels tend to lead people to do things they wouldn't necessarily do at home."*

—Hotelier Andre Balazs, the man behind London's Chiltern Firehouse

BEAUMONT A relative newcomer, this hotel caused a lot of media fuss when it opened because of the dramatic restoration of a former rental-car garage into a towering grand dame–style Art Deco hotel. The architects cleverly retained the ground-floor façade with its distinctive floor-to-ceiling steel casement windows, which date from 1927, but recreated the rest so that it is new but looks like a hotel from roughly the same period. There is sophistication in spades here, but there is also whimsy. This is most apparent in the concept behind the interior design, which was inspired by a fictional gentleman called 'Jimmy Beaumont', who left New York to open the Beaumont as an Anglo-American hotel prior to World War II; grand enough to attract high society but affordable enough to appeal to the middle classes too. The interior certainly reflects the style of a certain kind of gentleman: chequerboard lobby floor, early-20th-century paintings, gleaming period antiques. You'll think you've fallen into a Ralph Lauren ad. Rooms are spacious and sophisticated, but it's the little touches that win you over here. For example, the astonishing collections of books in each suite is curated by Heywood Hill bookstore nearby. The bookshop works closely with the hotel to find interesting books on intriguing Londoners and the city's history. It's just one way this place stands apart. But there are, oh, so many more.

Brown Hart Gardens, Mayfair, London.

HOTEL COSTES Set to be one of the newest hotels to hit London in late 2016, this is the sister venue of the near-cult Paris hotel of the same name run by the Costes brothers, which is a magnet for glam types who fly in and out for Paris Fashion Weeks and other super-stylish soirees. The Paris Hôtel Costes has been described as a 'sexy velvet boudoir' where beautiful people flock for 'lounging, posing, and listening to the smooth tunes of celeb DJ Stéphane Pompougnac'. While that's a little over the top (the hotel is also a great place for lunch; no posing required), the description does touch on the louche luxe decorating style that the hotel has become famous for. It's not known whether the London version will be done in the same opulent, decadent way, but it will likely be the same designer—Jacques Garcia—who does it, and he's not known for minimalism. So get out your velvet to wear. The hotel is set to be in a converted Victorian apartment building at One Sloane Gardens, just around the corner from Sloane Square. Work on the building—designed by Liberty architect Edwin Thomas Hall—is expected to start shortly, with the hotel due to open in 2016.

1 Sloane Gardens (Sloane Square), Chelsea, London.

Opposite *The bar and restaurant at The Gore are always popular with those attending concerts at the Royal Albert Hall*

THE LASLETT HOTEL There has been a lot of murmuring about this newish hotel, which only opened in late 2015, on blogs and travel forum. It seems to be one of the 'in' hotels, as much for its attention to books and literary references as for its fantastic location in the middle of Notting Hill. Spread across five magnificent mansions, it's a lush retreat from the madness of the Portobello Road markets, but it has drawn on the character of the latter to create rooms that are artistic and interesting. As the hotel states, it's more of a neighbourhood 'hangout' than a hotel, with a foyer that incorporates a library filled with art and design books, walls full of art, and even a shop featuring pieces from designers and artists. There's also a bar serving craft beers and locally sourced treats. It's all very Notting Hill. And all very engaging. Book lovers will adore the piles of vintage Penguins in the rooms, and the Harland Miller paintings on the wall, while antiques lovers and others searching for vintage treasures will relish the proximity to Portobello Road, still one of the best places to source great old finds.

8 Pembridge Gardens, Notting Hill, London.
www.living-rooms.co.uk/hotel/the-laslett

ZETTER TOWNHOUSE MARYLEBONE Fans of the Zetter Townhouse Clerkenwell will no doubt be looking forward to trying out its new sister hotel, the Zetter Townhouse Marylebone, a small but fiercely chic 24-bedroom property in a Georgian townhouse on Marylebone's Seymour Street. The original Zetter quickly gathered a following for its style (Cecil Beaton meets flea market meets crazy country house party), and the new Zetter looks like being just as fun, with antique furniture, rich velvet fabrics, hand-painted wallpaper and an inviting colour palette of tomato red, white, turquoise and navy. There's also a cosy restaurant called Seymour's Parlour, which is decorated in a rich palette of red and gold, features walls full of prints, paintings and trinkets, and offers dishes from renowned French chef Bruno Loubet. It's a great spot, whether it's for breakfast, cocktails or an intimate dinner. The hotel's interior designer, Russell Sage, was inspired by Sir John Soane's architectural collections and the hotel is crammed full with whimsical pieces. There are seven categories of rooms, although the top pick would be the Rooftop Apartment, which occupies the whole of the top floor and has its own private staircase, dressing room and a roof terrace with an outdoor bath. But the best bit about this gem is the location; right in the heart of Marylebone's fantastic shopping quarter.

28–30 Seymour Street, Marylebone, London.
www.thezettertownhouse.com

UNIQUE LODGINGS

13 PRINCELET STREET If you're a family or group of four and you love history, consider staying in a Landmark Trust property. The Trust restores graceful, beautiful or characterful buildings all over Great Britain and Europe in order to preserve them for future generations. Once the restorations have been completed, the properties are then opened to the public for short stays so that everyone may experience, for a short time, life in these remarkable buildings. There are only a few in London, but 13 Princelet Street is one to consider. This handsome house was built in 1718 to accommodate the influx of French Huguenots escaping religious persecution at home. Weavers—with their babies asleep under the looms—would have worked from what is now the upstairs bedroom. In 2004, the house was bequeathed to the Landmark Trust by its owner Peter Lerwill, an underwriter for Lloyd's, who had spent several years restoring and living in it. Thankfully, he retained much of the original character of the elegant four-storey building, including its original floor plan and also much of its interior, including the simple panelling, partitions and other joinery. The kitchen is a charming room done in an elegant eau-de-Nil shade (duck egg blue), while the other rooms are equally joyous in various shades of pale turquoise, the best colour to show the gilt-framed paintings, mirrors and gleaming antique furniture. Architecture fans will love it. It feels very modern (almost Scandinavian) while still clearly being a charming snapshot of history. The house has a stillness that's very calming, yet there's also the slight feeling that there could be someone in the rooms when you open the door. If you have a group, it's fantastically affordable: four nights start from £744. The bedrooms are a tad austere, but the living rooms are beautiful. Outside, London seems a long, long way away.

13 Princelet Street, Spitalfields, London. www.landmarktrust.org.uk

40 WINKS Located in East London, in a circa-1717 Queen Anne townhouse that's also the home of interior designer David Carter, 40 Winks offers just two beautiful bedrooms for guests to stay in. It's intimate, but enthralling, especially the interior design. The townhouse was used as a location house for many years and appeared in, a number of fashion and celebrity photo shoots. But it in 2009 David Carter decided to relaunch it as a place where creatives such as designers, artists, photographers and so forth could come and stay; a home away from home, if you like. The style is geared towards the dramatic and theatrical, and it certainly appeals to those working in art, design and the magazine industry. It's not for everyone, but there are many who will love its novelty.

109 Mile End Road, Stepney Green. www.40winks.org

KLASINA Sometimes travellers don't want to bed down in an ordinary hotel bed. Sometimes people want to try something different, just for the thrill. If you want to break up the monotony of hotel blandness, whether it's because you have kids, or a new partner, or just want a different experience, this is the destination for you. Klasina is a lovely old barge moored in the Docklands, a few minutes' walk from Canary Wharf. It's the home of Polly Dickens, the former creative director of Conran, and furniture designer Mark Gilbey, who happily rent out the spare bedroom to adventurous travellers, however, they can also be persuaded to rent out the whole thing if you prefer some privacy. My tip is to stay on the boat with the couple, as they're wonderful conversationalists, and Polly Dickens has a passion for food. She'll happily cook your eggs and ginger bacon in the morning, and tell you all the great places to go in London. They have dogs, too, so if you love the company of furry creatures, you'll adore it. And there's nothing nicer than sitting on a boat looking down at the Thames, reading a book or flicking through your iPad while the water laps at the bow. A great experience and even greater value.

Blackwall Basin, Canary Wharf, London. klasina.com

THE GRAZING GOAT Marylebone is a much-loved neighbourhood for the fashion and style set for its many boutiques, so it's strange that there are so few design-focused hotels in this neighbourhood. The Chiltern Firehouse opened in 2015, but until then, stylish places to stay were few and far between. Well, the Grazing Goat is adding to the quotient. This elegant, under-the-radar place is perfect for guests who don't like the fuss and bother that can be experienced in large hotels. For a start, it's hidden away in a side street that looks more like a village than a London scene, and the feeling of being a hotel anomaly becomes even stronger when you walk in the door, see the décor, and think you've been transported to an upmarket gastropub in the Cotswolds. The rooms are actually upstairs, and feel even more tranquil and inviting than the bar below. The subdued grey palette and Scandi-style fittings feel very modern and yet the timber touches and striped canvas blinds feel very English. A warning though: it IS first and foremost a pub (albeit a pub with gorgeous rooms), so you may hear people laughing in the distance and leaving at night. If you're worried, ask for a quieter suite. On the upside, you only need to go downstairs to get a decent meal! And breakfast, served in the ground-floor bar, includes such morning cocktails as Bellinis and Bloody Marys. Now how many hotels happily organise that?

6 New Quebec St, Marylebone, London. www.thegrazinggoat.co.uk

THE FIELDING Australian travellers love this place, which is something of a secret hideaway. Set in the heart of Covent Garden, right opposite the Royal Opera House, it's a little cutie that offers some of the prettiest rooms in the West End. And it's cheap as chips! OK, not always, but often. (Try Booking.com for the best prices.) If you're new to London, this is the kind of hotel you've always imagined; tucked down an enchanting pedestrian lane lit by Victorian gas lamps, and heralded by a gorgeous Georgian exterior—bright with window boxes during the day and boldly lit by fairy lights at night. There are no public rooms, and no breakfast either, but don't let either of those things dissuade you, because the atmosphere is like being in a private home. The best room is the pink one with the free-standing bath, but many others are just as lovely. (Note: They are on the simple side, so if you're used to Firmdale Hotel–style comfort, this hotel may not be for you.) The downside is that keys are handed in each time a guest leaves the hotel, but collecting them again is a lesson in English conviviality; the reception staff love to see how your day has been and whether they can help with recommendations for great restaurants, shops or places to go in the evening. The tight passages (watch the staircase!) and quirkiness isn't for everyone, but if you're after a lovely budget hideaway in an ideal location, you can't go past this treasure.
4 Broad Court, Covent Garden, London. www.thefieldinghotel.co.uk

THE FOX & ANCHOR The idea of staying in a posh pub has caught on in the past few years, mostly because it's usually cheaper than a hotel and you can go straight downstairs for a drink or dinner at the end of the day, and then hobble back to your stylish-but-cheap room upstairs, tired but content. However, the trick is the find the right hotel. Some, despite their interior design, stink of Guinness and nights that are best forgotten. But there are others that are as sweetly designed as anything hotelier Kit Kemp could dream up. The Fox & Anchor is one. Technically, this is a pub but it's actually more of a lovely, old-fashioned kind of inn—the kind England used to have decades ago—with a bar attached, rather than a pub with rooms on top. You can tell this by the textiles and furnishings. There are lots of gorgeous Arts and Crafts patterns, old mahogany doors, beautiful etched glass and lots of brass. Rooms feature architectural studies of local buildings, free-standing or copper bath-tubs, and a dark, masculine palette. It's all very dignified but very sexy too. Even the rooms have deep velvet sofas at the foot of the bed. If you love a beer at the end of a day of walking around London, staying somewhere like this would suit you perfectly. Cheap too, with rooms from £95.
115 Charterhouse Street, Clerkenwell, London. www.foxandanchor.com

THE FOX CLUB The Fox Club is not your typical hotel or club, that's for sure. Tucked away in a small side street in Mayfair, not too far off Piccadilly, this 18th-century townhouse hides nine exquisitely decorated rooms, but it also doubles as a members' club that's open to the public, with a bar, restaurant and function room. The club was named after Charles Fox, one of England's greatest bon vivants of the 18th century (as well as a statesman, but let's not let the facts get in the way of a good story). This residence was the house of Elizabeth Armistead, his mistress and eventually wife and, in fact, all of the bedrooms at the Fox Club are named after her lovers. Interesting, indeed. The rooms are fun, the design is even more irresistible, but it's the great location in the very heart of Mayfair (Buckingham Palace and Green Park are within touching distance) that will really pull you in.
46 Clarges Street, London. www.foxclublondon.com

THE ROOKERY The Rookery Hotel's rooms are as quirky and as beautiful as the building. This is not a place for minimalist or pragmatists to come; it is for those who cherish eccentricity, history, mystery, antiques and eclecticism. Which is many of us. The idea for the hotel came from two friends, Peter McKay and Douglas Blain, founding members of the Spitalfields Trust, a charity dedicated to restoring Georgian houses. What if, they thought, they could restore a cluster of period houses where people could stay? Somewhere that felt like more like a home than a hotel? And so began the task of fixing up these three derelict properties. The result is a sublime hideaway with a labyrinthing interior of flagstone floors, wood panels, and fantastic rooms decked out in rich colours, sumptuous textiles, elegant antiques and oil paintings and mad bathrooms with original features and witty plumbing. The best room, possibly the most eccentric room in all London, is the extraordinary top-floor, split-level Rooks' Nest, with its mezzanine floor, huge four-poster bed, 12-metre (40-foot) octagonal spire (revealed when you touch a button that moves the ceiling), *trompe l'oeil* and Turkey carpets, plus an Edwardian bath on a raised plinth in one corner. All absurdly romantic, but sentimentalists will love it. (So will kids!)
12 Peter's Lane, Cowcross Street, London. www.rookeryhotel.com

GREAT LITTLE CHEAPIES

KENSINGTON HOUSE HOTEL This nondescript little gem of a hotel not only has one of the best locations in London—right opposite Kensington Palace and Kensington High Street—but it also opens up to reveal a fantastic little hideaway. The downstairs entrance hall is light, welcoming and offers great free breakfasts in a sunny and spacious dining room, while the rooms are comfortable, no-nonsense affairs that will suit those who care more about their budgets than staying in a fancy design hotel. Everything is clean, neat-as-a-pin and, if you opt for a suite, you'll likely get a second room or a pretty bay window—and all for very little money. The best specials here are the 3-for-2 night deals, which are on offer all year, with single rooms starting from just £70 per night. (Doubles from £90.) The nearby neighbourhood, which encompasses lovely Launceston Place, pretty Kynance Mew and the gorgeous Gloucester Road area as well as bustling Kensington High Street, is also wonderful for basing yourself, especially in spring and summer when all the gardens of the houses around the hotel are in full bloom. But the most alluring part is the location. For the price, it's an incredible little hotel. Let's hope nobody finds out about it and the rates don't go up!

15–16 Prince of Wales Terrace, Kensington, London. www.kenhouse.com

THE CRANLEY This hotel is a little charmer. Hidden away in a quiet, dignified street of South Kensington, it's a pretty boutique number that promises a lot—and delivers. From the irresistible Wedgwood-blue foyer with its bookcases, fireplace and courtesy cocktails to the beautiful suites (many with antique four-poster beds and white marble bathrooms), everything here smacks of lovely, old-fashioned English elegance. OK, some parts are a little creaky and worn, and some guests complain of less-than-stellar service and cleanliness, but most people adore it. (It's not a five-star so don't expect Four Seasons standards.) It must be doing something right because TabletHotels.com has it on their books and they only accept premium properties. If you want a memorable, quintessential English hotel in the heart of London, one that respects history and nostalgia in its interior design and style, and tries very, very hard for its guests—and doesn't charge an arm and a leg for the service, either—this is the place to come. It's just lovely. A lot of charm for relatively little cash.

10 Bina Gardens, South Kensington, London. www.cranleyhotel.com

Right *The pink- and pistachio-coloured parlour at Number Sixteen hotel, South Kensington*

This page clockwise from left *The Chiltern Firehouse in Marylebone; Dickie Fitz; Pret-a-Portea at The Berkely*
Opposite clockwise from top *The Thomas Cubitt in Pimlico; Peggy Porschen patisserie on Elizabeth Street in Pimlico; and The Orange pub in Pimlico*

BEAUTIFUL RESTAURANTS AND BARS

Nowhere in the world offers the diversity of food that London does. Or the kind of unusual and beautifully designed dining spaces that it's served in. Witness the popularity of Skye Gyngell's former restaurant at Petersham Nurseries, which was set in the dirt-floored conservatory in a rustic garden nursery at the very edge of the city in leafy, bucolic Richmond. The menus were so innovative that Skye eventually, deservedly, won a Michelin star. Unfortunately, she then found it was, in her words, "a curse" because the snobbier part of the international restaurant set then flocked to the place and complained about sitting on rickety garden seats and getting—horror—dirt on their custom-made Italian shoes and designer bags. So she quietly handed the reigns of Petersham over, had a rest for a period, and is now happily ensconced in the bold, bright restaurant that is Spring, in Somerset House. There, her cuisine is still reminiscent of Petersham Nurseries, with eye-catching assemblies of beautiful seasonal ingredients strewn with flowers and herbs, and the interior still has the joyous feel of an orangery, but without the potted geraniums and plants, the zinc- and marble-topped garden tables, and absolutely no dirt, which many of her fans actually miss! The atmosphere isn't quite the same, but the food is still superb.

Then, there is Yotam Ottolenghi, the chef with a master's degree in philosophy and comparative literature who worked as a journalist before retraining for his current career. Mr Ottolenghi has put the pizzazz back into pomegranates and the bold back into butternut squash by reinventing vegetable dishes so they're unapologetically big and loud and (as he says) "noisy". He and his team started with a small gourmet deli, expanded to several more, then opened a restaurant NOPI and now have cookbooks and an expanding worldwide reputation. And while he does appreciate meat, he will always be known as the 'man who sexed up vegetables'. It's almost ironic that he found success in a city famous for its love of the Sunday roast. His restaurants are as sleek and as chic as the vegetable dishes he serves in them. You'll never look at broccoli the same way again.

And then, of course, there are the places where the atmosphere almost overshadows the food, such as the Dean Street Townhouse. One writer, Lisa Borgnes Giramonti, called the Dean Street Townhouse's restaurant "a sexy, velvety feast of a place that makes you want to drape yourself across a chaise, purr like Eartha Kitt and order a drink like whiskey, just to feel like a grown up". The restaurant, decorated in hues of petrol blue, olive green and Bloody Mary red, is certainly an escape from the inner-city cacaphony and it certainly entices you to order something elegant and strong and converse (or try to) in a witty or scintillating way. Not surprisingly, it's a firm favourite with the fashion, design, TV and media set.

Sitting alongside these legendary establishments are places such as Sketch, which has elevated restaurant design to a whole other level of experience. Yes, it has a fancy, two-Michelin-starred restaurant, but fans tend to gravitate to Glade, the woodland-themed lunch venue designed by textile artist Carolyn Quartermaine, or the Parlour, an eccentric patisserie, restaurant and bar decked out in pinks, oranges and dogtooth

prints (and a lot of crushed velvet!). Altogether, the venue comprises two critically acclaimed restaurants, an art gallery, a *salon de thé* and two spectacular bars. This place is so fashionable that it's been covered in a lot of media, but the design is still something you need to see at least once. (And if you feel faint from the prices, there are plenty of antique chaises to sink into.)

And then there were the restaurants that were too flamboyant, even for London's dandies. Les Trois Garçons was a former East End pub that was converted, with the help of a truckload of antiques, into a theatrical dining experience, where chandeliers and handbags dangled from the ceiling (a kind of style installation, or perhaps a fashion statement?), and the whole place had a storybook vibe that reflected its owners' private flat upstairs, where vintage frocks, sculptures and chaises longues ruled the rooms. (Even the loo was constructed out of an old Savoy lift rescued from a salvage yard.) Gwyneth Paltrow, Nicole Kidman and Madonna were said to be fans. Sadly, it's no longer in business, but thankfully, London still has enough fantastic restaurant spaces to keep us all entertained.

Even the more casual dining venues in London are now mini portraits of style that serve great food alongside gorgeous aesthetics. The Orange pub in Pimlico is deservedly popular for its elegantly simple interior; The Natural Kitchen in Marylebone is always bustling for its rustic charm and delicious dishes and takeaways, and wine bars/restaurants such as Carvosso's and Bumpkin in South Kensington are chic and cosy, especially on cold nights.

If you're looking for a memorable dining experience that combines good design (be it spectacular or quirky and cute) with delicious dishes, here are a few places to stir your imagination, from the lesser-known to the grand and glamorous.

Opposite from left to right *The pub known as Paradise by Way of Kensal Green; the Balcon Bar at the Sofitel St James*
This page *The David Collins-designed Artesian at the Langham Hotel*

ANDREW EDMUNDS There is just one word to describe this place: patina. It's very *World of Interiors*. But the media crowd loves it because the wine list is one of the best in London. It's the kind of place where you can easily right off an entire afternoon. But it's difficult to find. It's situated in an atmospheric 17th-century Hogarthian-ish townhouse deep in Soho, and so tiny you could easily miss it walking past. (Look for the charcoal-black façade and windows that are so charming they look like a film set.) The restaurant grew out of Mr Edmunds' antique prints business next door, and the interior retains the feel of an old antique map shop: bare wood floors, timber ceiling, rickety tables, candles in bottles, and paper tablecloths and napkins. As I said: lots of patina! The place has a well-deserved reputation for romance, but that's more to do with the fact that its interior is small and dark and tight (lots of leaning and squeezing here!) so that if you were sitting any nearer to your companion, you'd be on top of them. The menu, while short, is very, very good. But most regulars come here for the plonk. The wondrous wine list makes most oenophiles weak at the knees. (One wine is described as "ripe apricots, peaches, blossom and cream.") It's all so dark and clandestine and cosy that it feels like some secret society. Note: If you feel cramped in the downstairs area, ask if there's a table upstairs: that's where the better seating is. But far less atmosphere.
46 Lexington Street, Soho, London. www.andrewedmunds.com

ARCHIPELAGO Archipelago's mantra is 'exploring the exotic', and they certainly do that. Coming here is almost better than sailing a tall ship to Raja Ampat. Step inside this moodily lit space adorned with palms and peacock feathers and you'll find all manner of exotic fare to feed upon, from crocodile to wildebeest, garlic crickets and even scorpion. (No sign of the tarantulas to be found in the markets of Cambodia, but perhaps there's a limit, even for Archipelago.) Diners say it's popular for romantic nights (the walls are as red as the blood in a New Guinea cannibal's soup). One fan claimed it's a great first-date venue because there are so many conversation starter props to keep the chat going if the date falls flat. But people don't come here for the intimacy. (Honestly, you'd have more chance of that on the M1.) No, this is a place to push the old taste buds; see if they're still up for a challenge. There are chocolate-dipped locusts and honey-poached bees. Plus bunny chow (!), and kangaroo, and zebra and pythons, too. Not surprisingly, vegetarians may find it all a bit much, but the adventurous diners will love it.
53 Cleveland Street, Fitzrovia, London. www.archipelago-restaurant.co.uk

Andrew Edmunds is a humble, endearingly no-nonsense bistro in Soho that serves up consistently satisfying dishes—and has a legion a fans to prove it.

72 **ARTESIAN** Winner of the World's 50 Best Bars awards four years in a row, Artesian at the Langham Hotel was designed by the late, great David Collins and his studio team, and is a glamorous space that makes you feel you should be wearing a sheath of silk and ordering expensive French champagne. Designed to be a Victorian cabinet of curiosities, it mixes aesthetic styles with fabulous panache. There's pagoda bar (the shape of which is echoed in the chandeliers), bespoke lacquers that reference *la chasse aux papillons*, silver-leaf *boiserie*, clamshell-shaped tub chairs upholstered in pale pink and lavender leather (crocodile print no less, although it's leather made to look like croc, not the real stuff!) and jewelled mirror panelling. Drop in mid-afternoon for a little aperitif—the cocktails are just as exotic as the décor—and marvel at the gorgeousness of it all. As bars go, it's all decadent, every last inch of it.

1C Portland Place, Regent Street, London. www.artesian-bar.co.uk

BALTHAZAR The original Balthazar in New York has been one of Manhattan's top dining spots for some years now, and this new London outpost hopes to capitalise on the success across the pond. It's decorated in the same classic, Parisian-brasserie-style elegance, and features good ol' Frenchy dishes to match. It's pretty, there's no doubt about it, but whether it becomes as much of a dining cult as its cousin on the other side of the Atlantic remains to be seen. Francophiles will certainly love it.

4–6 Russell Street, Soho, London. www.balthazarlondon.com

CLARIDGE'S AND FUMOIR There are those who always love a grande-dame hotel, and London has some of the grandest dames in the world. One of the best is Claridge's Art Deco hotel, where the tiny, but very splendid Fumoir bar will always offer a memorable evening. With its dark timber, its shimmering mirrored surfaces and its silvery glow, it's a gorgeous place to catch up with friends. Or to simply sit with someone special and celebrate the magic that is London. The centerpiece is William Klein's portrait from 1956 of Lisa Fonssagrives blowing smoke through a black veil, which has been blow up and hung behind the marble bar. That's the first sign you're in a stylish joint! The second is the sight of the tiers of premium tipple—there are no bargain bottles here. (And most is more than 40 per cent proof, too!) The third (if you need a third) is the fact that everyone is dressed up. Like adults. High heels and all. It's that kind of place. You don't really schlepp in after a day doing the sales at Marks and Spencer. But perhaps the best things about this sexy bolthole are (a) the Lalique crystal glasses, and (b) the size of the place. It only fits two dozen or so into its oh-so-cosy tables and horseshoe bar, so it immediately feels convivial. Just don't jerk your head when a Hollywood star or big name walks in; it's a favourite hangout for those who are often seen in *Vanity Fair*.

49 Brook Street, Mayfair, London. www.claridges.co.uk

DICKIE FITZ The quirky name is very Australian (it's named after Fitzrovia, the area in which it's located), but the design and dishes are most definitely on an international level. Banana yellow banquets and dandelion-style lighting reflect the Pacific-inspired cuisine, which includes fantastic fish dishes, while the Art Deco staircase adds a note of elegance. The Antipodean heritage of the head chef is clear, but there's a lot of London here, too.

48 Newman Street, Fitzrovia, London. www.dickiefitz.co.uk

DUKES BAR It was at Dukes Bar that James Bond's creator Ian Fleming felt inspired to create his iconic cocktail. Today, Dukes' head bartender, Alessandro Palazzi, still makes the best martinis in London , using (wait for this) lemons imported from the Amalfi just that day. That's the kind of bar you want. All class. Don't miss a peek at the Champagne Lounge; decorated in shades of sherbert pink and lime, it's the opposite of Bond and more like the haunt of a Bond girl such as Pussy Galore.

35 St. James Place, Mayfair, London. www.dukeshotel.com

LE CHANDELIER TEA HOUSE Le Chandelier looks like a very stylish vintage store, crossed with a very pretty patisserie. It's a little over the top, but that's the point; it's not designed for minimalists. The roof drips in glistening French and Italian chandeliers, (also available for purchase if you so desire), which light up the tables in a glamorous way. Underneath them, there are gorgeous velvet wingback armchairs to sink into, a sublime French-grey baker's table groaning with delish goodies (from meringues to cheesecakes to Portuguese custard tarts), and antique doors, gilded mirrors and artwork lining the walls. As for tea: there more than 30 varieties, elegantly presented in glass jars. Nab the pale-green velvet sofa if you can; it's exquisite. (Note: Many have said service isn't great, so take a mag while you wait!)

161 Lordship Lane, East Dulwich, London. www.lechandelier.co.uk

LES DEUX SALONS Right in the heart of Covent Garden, close to that other Frenchy establishment Balthazar, Les Deux Salons offers fine French dining in a superbly stylish space, with interiors designed by Isabelle Chatel de Brancion and Terence Conran.

40–42 William IV Street, Covent Garden, London. lesdeuxsalons.com

MASSIMO'S A magnificent place, this restaurant was designed by the inimitable David Collins, who has sadly passed away but left an incredible legacy in all the bars and hotels he and his team designed. The dominant hues are navy blue (so British!), olive green and white and grey, which have been combined in theatrical striped columns, a marble bar, and buttoned banquettes. It's all very dignified, but also very pretty and witty in parts. (Note how the swirls on the floor elegantly match the wall mural and the arches in the ceiling.) It somehow manages to be both grand and welcoming; you'll happily walk in without being intimidated but may then find yourself straining your neck to admire all the architectural details rather than concentrating on the food and drinks.

Corinthia Hotel, 10 Northumberland Avenue, Whitehall, London. www.massimo-restaurant.co.uk

OTTOLENGHI Ottolenghi needs little introduction after the swathes that have been written about this new empire. Still incredible, still friendly, still reasonably priced. Go for the famous vegetable dishes, but also go for the ambience. Even if you're sitting at the bar, the vibe is good. Everything here is creative and contemporary, especially those window displays of colour and beauty! Oh! They really need to photograph them for the covers of the books. So much more eye-catching than a black frypan.

21–22 Warwick Street, Soho, London; 63 Ledbury Road, Notting Hill London W11; 87 Upper Street, Islington, London, and 13 Motcomb Street, Belgravia, London.

RESTAURANT STORY A must for those who like a little narrative with their food, or who like to know the origin of where their produce comes from, Restaurant Story is a brilliant idea that other chefs could do well to follow. The premise is really about the provenance of the food you're eating—"we seek to tell our story through the food we serve" say the restaurant's owners—but it's done in a far more creative way than simply listing the growers on the menu. In fact, the concept of 'story' has been taken down many layers, right to the conception of the cuisine. As RS explains: "dishes are inspired by memory, or provenance of ingredients." So, for example, the English pear, artichoke and verbena may be inspired by a summer spent in a villa in Tuscany. You get the picture. Everything you see, smell and taste on the plate is designed to take your senses back to a wonderful memory in life—or the chef's life (or both)—and it really does work. In fact, Restaurant Story has been so successful, not only in its narratives but its quality of dishes, that it gained a Michelin star only five months after opening. So, not such a gimmick, after all. Best of all, there's a giant book collection, which you can add to by bringing your own favourite read. Wonderful. Just wonderful. As the esteemed reviewer from Zagat said: "If you're longing for a visit to The Fat Duck [the acclaimed restaurant in Bray run by Heston Blumenthal], but don't want to make the trek, Story is the next best thing."

199 Tooley Street, Southwark, London. www.restaurantstory.co.uk

SARASTRO Years ago, I worked as a deputy editor on a London travel magazine. My editor was a former rock star (he is still famous in parts of Europe and elsewhere), who had left the stage to follow a career in journalism. He was still involved in the London music scene (and had some incredible stories to tell, especially about his former neighbour and 'acquaintance' Sid Vicious). Well, surprisingly, Sarastro was my rock-star editor's favourite place to take his rock-star friends. It's billed as an opera-themed, Mediterranean / Turkish restaurant on Drury Lane, but it's actually a lot more impressive than this karaoke-style tag suggests. The restaurant offers actual operatic performances by both professional singers and staff, most of whom are very, very good. If you can't afford the Royal Opera House in Covent Garden, this is the next best thing. Imagine listening to 'O Sole Mio' live while you're enjoying your Cloudy Bay and a bit of tasty brie? Magnificent. Even old rockers love it.

126 Drury Lane, Covent Garden, London. info@sarastro-restaurant.com

London dining runs from the eccentric to the elegant, and the casual to the fiercely sophisticated. However, some of the best food is hidden behind some of the most unassuming façades.

74

SKETCH Restraint is a banned word at Sketch, where the 'more is more' philosophy has been applied to the interior design. This wonderfully playful space that houses a tea room, lounge bar and two highly regarded restaurants, has been part of the Mayfair scene for 10 years now, but is still filling column inches in newspapers and on the internet for its ever-evolving, hype-inducing design. There are several parts to this dining empire, each designed to appeal to different aesthetics. Glade is a painterly tea salon created by artists Carolyn Quartermaine and Didier Mahieu who took inspiration from early-20th-century stationery to design a delicate space that is part real, part fantasy. The walls are découpaged out of hundreds of metres of paper to create a storybook backdrop to a room that features charming, vintage 1950s rattan furniture, sourced in the south of France. The Gallery next door is just as sweet but designed in a completely different way by Paris-based designer India Mahdavi, who used sculptural chairs covered in fairy-floss-pink fabric to create a modern, yet girlie and flirtatious space to dine. And the Parlour is a bold collage of retro prints and red velvet that makes for a theatrical space to sip champagne and indulge in afternoon teas and decadent cakes. The crowd here (it's very 'scene-y') is often just as glamorous as the surroundings, especially in the sumptuous Lecture Room restaurant.
9 Conduit Street, Mayfair, London. www.sketch.london

THE CONNAUGHT The Connaught Bar at The Connaught Hotel is one of those very proper, very English old-guard bars, where white-gloved barmen wheel around a Martini trolley—complete with homemade bitters. It's the kind of bar where you do need to be appropriately dressed (even nice shoes will do), in order to feel like you're, well, appropriate for it. Interior designer David Collins is famous for creating London's most desirable watering holes and the Connaught Bar is no exception. It was apparently inspired by English Cubist and Irish art from the 1920s, and the silver leaf and dark leather interior does have an elegant, 1920s feel. However, the comfort is definitely 21st century, with deep, inviting couches and slick service. Americans have always loved the Connaught Hotel (they think it's *Downton Abbey*). Ralph Lauren even copied the staircase for his flagship New York store, while Gwyneth Paltrow and Chris Martin stayed in the Apartment for eight months. It's all very proper, and very English. There's even a shoe-shine chair on the first landing: £30 buys gentlemen a Lobb shoe shine (any leather shoes), a jacket pressing, and a cocktail while they wait. It's a nice touch, particularly for those meeting a first date or a special somebody in the bar.
Carlos Place, Mayfair, London.

THE MODERN PANTRY Everything about the Modern Pantry is thoughtfully done. For a start, the navy and off-white colour palette was inspired by Flora Danica, an atlas of indigenous Danish plant life catalogued in copper-engraved plates during the late 18th century, and later applied to a celebrated range of porcelain by Royal Copenhagen. Isn't that the most ingenious thing to begin your restaurant concept from? The nod to nature continues in framed images of New Zealand's plant life hung on the walls. And also in the cuisine, which is as fresh as a just-plucked herb from a Swedish summer garden. It's all very refreshing. And very, very lovely. But don't think it's a rustic greenhouse with ivy twining through the brickwork. Oh, no. This is as smart and as modern as a Danish supermodel. Housed in the impressive Grade–II listed Art Deco Alphabeta Building on the corner of Finsbury Square, the restaurant's interior is all understated elegance, with a solid oak bar set against whitewashed walls, and furniture from the Danish midcentury movement, with modernist chairs and tables, and bespoke glass pendant lighting by AvroKo. It's all clean lines and simplicity. Even the spaces are partitioned by stunning navy-and-gold moveable panels instead of walls. Design fans will adore it. Pure Danish class. In every way.

14 Finsbury Square, Finsbury Square, London; 47–48 St John's Square, Clerkenwell, London. www.themodernpantry.co.uk

THE IVY One of the West End's most beloved establishments, this enticing restaurant and drinking den has had a makeover recently, and the new look has tones of a slick, upmarket New York bar, particularly in the high bar seats and Hollywood banquettes. The bold palette comprises Kelly green, coral red, modern brass (very 'in' in the design world at present) and fantastic ceiling lights. It's cosy but not claustrophobic, casual but still smart enough for a hot date or girls' night. It's not surprising that the interior feels very 'Manhattan'; the overhaul was the result of New York–based design firm Martin Brudnizki Design Studio. There's also a sister Ivy on King's Road in Chelsea, which is more botanical in design, but no less beautiful.

1–5 West Street, Covent Garden, London. www.the-ivy.co.uk

Opposite *Sketch*
This page from left to right *The Connaught Bar; The almost theatrical-style stairwell of the pub known as Paradise by Way of Kensal Green, which looks like something Oliver Messel or Cecil Beaton might have dreamed up*

THE DUCK AND RICE The cutely named Duck and Rice is more of a gastropub but a very, very stylish one, with copper beer tanks and blue floral tiles inspired by Chinese ceramics. It actually dubs itself a "modern Chinese gastropub" (are there such things?), and it seems to fit perfectly into the environment of Soho, where Chinese restaurants and classic pubs sit side by side like old friends. The interior design is the world of Istanbul-based design studio Autoban, and it's beautiful. Your eyes may be drawn to the curves of the shiny copper beer vats first, but then they're likely to settle on the grand spiral staircase, and the huge blue and white ceramic wall panels, like blow-ups of willow patterns, which bring a certain sexiness to the ol' porcelain classic. It's a confusing space, with pub downstairs and restaurant upstairs, but follow your nose to the fantastic Chinese cuisine, and you'll be fine.

90 Berwick Street, Soho, London. www.theduckandrice.com

V&A'S MORRIS ROOM This may seem a strange inclusion, but design lovers will no doubt nod in agreement. The café / restaurant at the V&A (Victorian and Albert Museum) isn't the kind of place you go to for food—there are dozens of restaurants around South Kensington that offer more interesting cuisines—however, it IS somewhere you go to be inspired by design. Which is, after all, the whole point of the V&A. It comprises several spaces, but perhaps the most beautiful room to sit / dine in is the Morris Room: the William Morris–designed salon. It's a tranquil, heavenly treat of green and gold and wondrous William Morris patterns. (The deep colours show that he was still under the influence of the Gothic Revival at the time.) He embellished the walls with Elizabethan-style panelling and included a low relief of olive branches: both magnificent. Don't miss the stained-glass windows, too, which feature female figures painted by Edward Burne-Jones and Philip Webb.

Cromwell Road, South Kensington, London. www.vam.ac.uk

PARADISE BY WAY OF KENSAL GREEN This is a pub, but not as you know it. In fact, if you're more inclined to seek comfort in a simple old bar, this is probably not the place for you. It's an ornately decorated ode to high Victoriana, with gilt picture frames, decorative wallpaper, furniture more curvy than Sophie Dahl's body (she loves it here), and a stairwell that has to be seen to be believed, with an enormous crystal chandelier and ivy growing right through it. There are several spaces: two bars and a restaurant downstairs, and three further bars and a private dining room upstairs. It's a great place to spend an evening, squished in one of the cosy corners, getting slowly wasted on French champagne. Check the website for events: they often have life-drawing classes with burlesque dancers as models, and a once-a-month Saturday vintage sale.

19 Kilburn Road, Kensal Green, London. www.theparadise.co.uk

THE WOLSELEY A favourite for many, this esteemed Art Deco–style establishment housed in a former Jazz Age auto showroom has the glamour of the grand old café-brasseries in Paris and Venice. It's a marbled, mirrored, domed, Doric-columned black and white ode to good ol' class, and serves equally glamorous, equally classy entrées such as soufflé Suisse and croustade of quail eggs with hollandaise. (If you go for breakfast, they'll give you the *Financial Times* or the *New York Times* to read: it's that kind of place.) It's arguably one of the most beautiful dining spaces in London, and is so popular there's an online shop, so you can purchase the same silver-plate pepper mills and ice buckets.

160 Piccadilly, St James's, London. www.thewolseley.com.

WEST THIRTY-SIX Notting Hill is full of cosy boltholes that are perfect for a dark glass after a day battling the crowds at the Portobello Road markets. This rustic hideaway is one of them. There are walls made from well-aged timber planks, dark cabinetry full of books, chocolate leather armchairs, and lots of seating nooks to get comfy in, but they are spread across many levels, so always plenty of room. It's a quirky combination of funky and farmyard, with the old timbers and contemporary colours (peacock and lime green), but locals here love that sort of whimsy. Try and nab a seat on the outdoor terraces: lovely in the summer months.

36 Golborne Road, Notting Hill, London. www.w36.co.uk

BOTANICAL-INSPIRED DINING SPOTS

In the last few years, London has seen a proliferation of horticulturally themed dining places. The trend began with places such as Petersham Nurseries in Richmond, left, which went from being a rustic nursery café to a Michelin-starred establishment under Australian chef Skye Gyngell. (Gyngell now runs Spring in Somerset House, also botanically inclined). The botanical dining trend then spread to other neighbourhoods, and is most apparent in Chelsea, home of the Chelsea Flower Show. The Ivy, pictured this page, and the Botanist in Sloane Square are just two garden-inspired restaurants, with The Ivy going as far as designing its menus to look like authentic garden plans. The interior, meanwhile, is punctuated with botanical prints, and the colour palette is a summery combination of tangerine and green although the courtyard / garden is perhaps the prettiest place to dine when it's sunny. Other places to dine among the flowers are the Orangery in Kensington Gardens; the Rooftop Gardens on Kensington High Street; Bumpkin, which emulates the country look (various places in London); Clifton Nurseries in Maida Vale, and the flower-covered Churchill Arms pub in Kensington. There are also many more set within gardens, including the cafés of Regent's Park, the Garden History Museum, and Kew Botanic Gardens. Maggie Jones in Kensington is a lovely little place relished by locals for its cosy, romantic atmosphere as much as its baskets of flowers (dried and fresh). The place is designed to feel like a rustic barn, complete with faux beehive, but the food is anything but rough. Finally, Bourne & Hollingsworth in Clerkenwell has been popping up on blogs and Instagram posts for a year or two now, but it's still sweet, especially the petite conservatory full of ferns and floral armchairs. Farmhouse-inspired, yes, but it's still delicious and beautifully prepared.

This page from top to bottom *The Ivy in Chelsea; a street florist on Fulham Road, bright with Christmas blooms*
Opposite *The romantic greenhouses of Petersham Nurseries café*

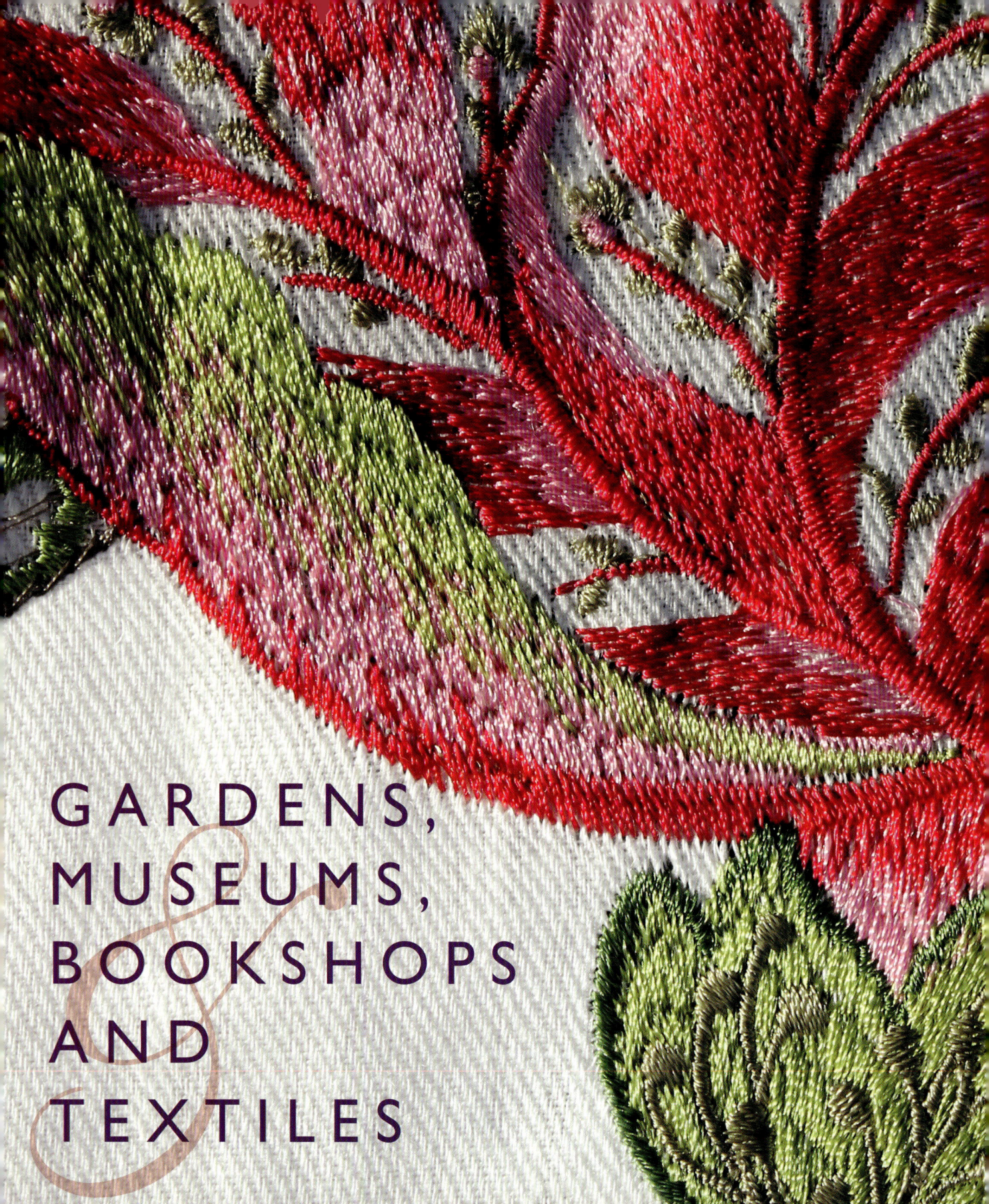

GARDENS,
MUSEUMS,
&
BOOKSHOPS
AND
TEXTILES

Clockwise from top left *Churchill Arms flowers; blossoms in spring; pavement outside a shop front in Pimlico—amazing!; the Babylon Roof Gardens; David Linley's store in Belgravia (Princess Margaret's son; he's also a famous furniture designer).*
Opposite *Babylon Roof Gardens*
Previous pages *Manuel Canovas fabrics at Colefax and Fowler*

BOTANICAL SPACES

BABYLON ROOF GARDENS (FORMERLY KENSINGTON ROOF GARDENS) Located high above the chain stores and pedestrian madness of Kensington High Street, this is one of London's most surprising gardens. Known as either the Babylon Roof Gardens or the Kensington Roof Gardens, this is Sir Richard Branson's private oasis, which he has graciously opened to the public. It's a remarkable space, carved out of the rooftop terrace of the old Derry and Toms department store. For many decades, this was the largest roof garden in Europe, and it still rates as one of the most spectacular. There are several parts to the garden: a Spanish garden, set out in a Moorish style based upon the Alhambra in Spain, with fountains, vine-covered walkways and Chusan palms; a Tudor style garden, characterised by its archways, secret corners, hanging wisteria, roses, lilies and lavender; and an English woodland garden, with more than 100 species of trees, a stream, and a garden pond that is the home to pintail ducks and four flamingos called Bill, Ben, Splosh and Pecks. There are more than 30 different species of trees in the woodland garden alone, including trees from the original planting more than 60 years ago, despite having only a metre of soil in which to grow. Although they are on a rooftop, the trees were made the subject of tree preservation orders in 1976. The entire garden was listed as a Grade II site by the English Heritage in 1978. Visitors are able to see it two ways: by booking a table in the restaurant or having a drink on the Babylon Terrace, or by asking to wander around the gardens on their own. It's normally open to the public at certain times during the week in summers, usually on weekends and one day during the week, but ring ahead to check opening times, and to see if there's a function, in which case it'll be closed to the public. The garden is accessed via Derry Street, through a doorway marked '99 Kensington High Street'. Ask the receptionist for further directions, but it's best to call first.

99 Kensington High Street, Kensington, London. (Via Derry Street.)
www.virginlimitededition.com/the-roof-gardens

CLIFTON NURSERIES This is the kind of garden and nursery you imagine having when you live in a city and dream of country getaways: white greenhouses groaning with grapevines and stacked with cute pots; a well-curated plant selection; topiaries to tease the eyes. There's also a delightful café, the Quince Tree Café, set in among the plants in a palm house, which serves breakfast, lunch and afternoon tea. If that wasn't enough to tempt you, there's a wonderful story behind it all. The nursery began life as a communal garden in 1851; an 'ornamental garden and nursery ground' with a private roadway between numbers 5 and 6 to allow access to it. The lease at the time stated that nothing could be built except greenhouses, preventing further development. Fast forward to 1879, when a new owner, Johannes Adam Krupp, took over the seven greenhouses, arranged the central fountain (a relic from the days when it was an ornamental garden), and tried to build a large cottage for his family. A solicitor's letter was duly sent to him reminding him of the original purpose of the land, and that no buildings were to be built other than garden ones. Clearly, this land was always destined to belong to gardeners. Fast forward again to the early 1900s, when Sydney Cohen takes over the lease, and Clifton becomes a thriving business. However, when he died suddenly of a heart attack, its future looked grim. So in stepped Lord Jacob Rothschild, a named inextricably linked to horticulture, who not only invested in this worn-out old nursery but ordered a spectacular new palm house and a lovely shop, plus a garden advice and a planning department. Since then, Clifton has won five Chelsea Gold medals and three Silver Gilts and become a noted name in the world of London gardening. Its original owner must be looking down from Horticultural Heaven and shaking his head with joy. We need more green-fingered saviours like this in the world.

5A Clifton Villas, Little Venice, London. www.clifton.co.uk

DUCK ISLAND COTTAGE Many people walk straight past the cottage and garden on Duck Island in St James's Park without even knowing it's there. It's a small but lovely garden with a rather unusual CV. The original cottage was erected in the 17th century, when St James's was the deer park for Whitehall Palace. The present cottage was built in the 19th century, in the style of a cottage *orné*, and the lovely, Arts and Crafts 'Cottage Garden' was added in the 20th century. The name came from the cottage's original use as a bird-keeper's house. During the time of King Charles II, the king had continued his grandfather's practice of keeping aviaries along Birdcage Walk, and had appointed Edward Storey as 'Keeper of the King's Birds'—which is still commemorated to this day by the 'Storey's Gate' entrance to the park. The island came to be known as Duck Island at the same time as the king created the post of 'Governor of Duck Island'; a keeper's position that came with a small salary but lots of garden and parkland! The gingerbread architecture, known as cottage *orné* style, was designed to contrast with the increasingly bland architecture of the government offices being erected in nearby Whitehall. Its decorative features include distinctive lozenge-latticed glazing bars, and a channel of water running beneath the rustic loggia. Today, it's used as the headquarters for the London Historic Parks and Gardens Trust. Unfortunately, the cottage is not open to the public, but the gorgeous Arts and Crafts garden, which is meticulously kept, can easily be viewed as you're wandering through St James's Park.

ITALIAN WATER GARDEN This garden is a 150-year-old ornamental water garden located on the north side of Kensington Gardens near Lancaster Gate. It's a small but beautiful part of this enormous green space (encompassing Kensington Gardens and Hyde Park), which few people realise exists. It was created in 1861 as a gift from Prince Albert to his beloved Queen Victoria. At the time, Prince Albert was a keen gardener, and had taken charge of the gardens at Osborne House on the Isle of Wight, where the royal family spent their holidays. One of the big changes Albert made was the introduction of an Italian garden with large raised terraces, fountains, urns and new geometric flower beds. He loved it so much, he wanted to do something similar in Kensington Gardens. The design he conceived for the latter was intended to incorporate four main 'basins', or large pools, with central rosettes, all elaborately carved in Carrara marble. He also commissioned a large stone and marble Tazza Fountain surrounded by intricately carved stone statues and five urns that featured five designs: a Swan's breast, a woman's head, a ram's head, a dolphin and an oval. On an early summer's morning, when the light is gentle, it's a serene place to wander. (It's also beautiful covered by snow in the depths of winter.) The garden is now listed Grade II by English Heritage as a site of particular importance. To find it, go to the northern part of Kensington Gardens, where it's situated at the head of the Long Water—the river that flows through Kensington Gardens into Hyde Park—at the part where it becomes the Serpentine. At the north of the gardens is the Pump House where you can see Queen Victoria and Prince Albert's initials on one of the walls. The building once contained a steam engine that operated the fountains, while the pillar on the roof is a cleverly disguised chimney.

Kensington Gardens, London.

NATURAL HISTORY MUSEUM WILDLIFE GARDEN Garden designer and author William Robinson first put forward the idea of making 'wild gardens' in London in 1870, but it was 100 years before the idea of using native plants to make wild oases in towns was really considered. In 1995, a wildlife garden was finally designed and created in the south-west corner of the Natural History Museum. It is now a delightful place to wander after walking through the museum, or to sit and contemplate your next step on your urban itinerary.

Cromwell Road, South Kensington, London. www.nhm.ac.uk

SCARLET AND VIOLET This is such a witty name for a florist, especially one that specialises in colour. And it's just as gorgeous as its name. In fact, it's so photogenic that it's been featured in countless magazine spreads and blog / Instagram posts. There's cute rustic benches groaning with vases and bouquets, lots of scented perfumes, porcelain, and even a quirky Citroen van. The service is superb and the flowers spectacular. Everything is creatively arranged, with pinks and red colours a favourite (not surprising, given the name). It's all beautiful, beautiful, beautiful.

76 Chamberlayne Road, Queen's Park, London. www.scarlet-violet. myshopify.com

From opposite left to right A Chelsea in Bloom *display;* Peony display in Chelsea; *a bouquet from* Wild at Heart *florist;* Wild at Heart *florist* **Following pages** *Florist at Launceston Place*

*"London is the world's garden capital—
just as Los Angeles is its film capital,
and Paris its fashion capital ..."*

—Garden designer Tom Turner

CHELSEA IN BLOOM If you happen to find yourself in London in the week of May when the Chelsea Flower Show is on (usually the third week in May), and you have a spare hour or two, take the tube to Sloane Square. There, you'll be rewarded with one of the most sublime sights in London at this time of year: streets and streets full of boutiques displaying magnificent floral arrangements. It's all part of the ingenious Chelsea in Bloom festival, which is run during the same week as the Chelsea Flower Show, and designed to complement it. How it works is that all the shops in and around Sloane Square, Sloane Street and the Duke of York Square are invited to decorate their fronts (and sides) with plants and flowers as a celebration of the spirit of the nearby Chelsea Flower Show. There is always a theme, and the displays are then judged by an expert judging panel from the Show. There is also a People's Champion Award, which people vote for online. In 2015, the theme was 'Fairy Tales', and boutiques such as Jo Malone, Fendi, Lulu Guinness, Browns, Escada, Rag and Bone, Emma Hope, LK Bennett, Club Monaco, Smythson, and the competition winner Kate Spade garlanded their exteriors in magical, mythical displays. There are complimentary guided tours, which start at Sloane Square, or you can download a map and walk the route yourself. There is also a pop-up champagne bar and a fairy-tale forest in Sloane Square. It's almost as good as the Chelsea Flower Show itself, and the best thing is, it's completely free! There's also Belgravia in Bloom and Pimlico in Bloom, two 'sister' festivals that have sprung up in recent years. Look for the maps of all the participating stores in many of the boutiques.

www.chelseainbloom.co.uk

Opposite *The Kate Spade fashion boutique on Sloane Square always creates eye-catching, botanical-themed windows and displays for the Chelsea in Bloom festival in May, which coincides with the Chelsea Flower Show. Here, the florists at Wild at Heart (which is located in nearby Pimlico) have turned exotic flowers into a giant toucan for the façade of the store.*
This page clockwise from top left *Purple palette of orchids in Chelsea, a detail of the Kate Spade store, Hackett (upmarket men's store in Chelsea), and another Chelsea in Bloom creation on Sloane Square.*

of Useful Plants

PAPER, ROPE
& FABRIC

Plants processed for
their strong and often
lightweight fibres

CHELSEA PHYSIC GARDEN The Chelsea Physic Garden was founded in 1673 by the Society of Apothecaries as a working garden to grow and trial *materia medica*, or plants designed for medical and scientific purposes. The name was eventually changed to 'physic' to reflect its primary use as a herb garden with medicinal plants. It was located in a large walled enclosure near the Thames, creating a microclimate that was perfect for growing plants that wouldn't normally survive in a London winter. Fast forward a few centuries to today and not only does the garden still survive in the middle of an over-developed London (a feat in itself), but it is one of the most enchanting green spaces in the city. The entrance to it is on Swan Walk, through a discreet iron gate in a high brick wall that's half-hidden by foliage—which gives you an indication of the magic to come. Once inside, the garden opens out to a wondrous space that looks and feels more like an Arts and Crafts country garden than an educational space. However, it's very much a botanical garden, where all the plants are named and explained. There are plants for dyes, plants for scent, plants for all kinds of ailments. Even the trees are beautiful. (Don't miss the handkerchief tree that overhangs the main lawn and the purple Tamerisk tree when it's in full bloom.) The garden and its labels encourage visitors to bend down and sniff or touch plants, and serious visitors with notebooks pore over the beds, noting down the precise botanical name of plants they love and hope to order later. There are around 5000 edible, medicinal and other useful plants, plus a lovely café, the Tangerine Dream, to sit in afterwards, contemplating it all. It's a wonderful place to wander on a sunny day (or even an overcast one!) learning about the secrets of plants and their many uses. Even nongardeners will appreciate the tranquillity.

66 Royal Hospital Road, Chelsea, London. chelseaphysicgarden.co.uk

COS&TRUMP   *146*   Kee

COLUMBIA ROAD Columbia Road is famous for its colourful, open-air flower market, with its potted pleasures and swathes of bouquets. Perhaps the most popular stall is the geranium stall, which often sees people gather five deep to choose a pot or three. However, the street is more than a line of characterful flower sellers. There are also several great indie boutiques here, a lovely store called the Open House Garden Shop (at 120 Columbia Road) selling all manner of covetable gardening stuff, as well as some cute cafés to have lunch at afterwards. Note: The flower market is only open on Sundays, until 2pm or 3pm.

GARDEN MUSEUM Several friends had suggested the Garden Museum wasn't worth seeing. "There's not a lot to it, other than some antique tools and old photos, a garden bookshop, a parterre garden and a cute café," said one. Well, that sounded just perfect to me. So I hailed a cab to visit one day. "The Garden Museum?" queried the driver, enthusiastically. "That's my favourite place in London! It's a fantastic secret. I like to go there when I'm having a bad day. There's a lovely café where you can eat your lunch in a garden and it feels like a million miles away." Now London cabbies are some of the savviest folks in the city, so I raised my hopes. Just after Lambeth Palace Gardens, he let me out at a charming little chapel on the riverside. "Just in there," he said nodding cheerily. "You're gonna have a lovely time." And then drove away, leaving me in a part of London I'd never been in all the years I've lived in this city. Inside the chapel, the museum seemed to consist of a bookstore full of garden books, a little café, an exhibition of garden embroidery and a desk with three cheery ladies. "Just up the stairs here," replied Cheery Lady Number One. "And don't forget to look at our parterre garden too; it's just come into bloom." Well the Garden Museum was small, but if you love gardens and the history of gardens, it's absolutely fascinating. It occupies what was the parish church of St Mary-at-Lambeth and the burial ground of two famous 17th-century royal gardeners and plant hunters: John Tradescant the father and his son of the same name. Inside, the permanent collections include antique garden tools (daisy grubbers and other unusual things), photos of gardeners through the decades, and even an authentic old Yates seed dispenser from a department store display. After you've seen an exhibition, the garden bookshop is a wonderful place to browse, with vintage and new titles on gardening, and gifts galore. I picked up a copy of the limited edition catalogue of the museum's hugely successful exhibition *Fashions and Gardens*, which was curated by writer and museum trustee Nicola Shulman, wife of the 5th Marquess of Normanby and sister of British *Vogue* editor Alexandra Shulman (who naturally featured it in a *Vogue* issue). It's a thoughtfully curated bookshop, full of unusual titles and lovely ideas for gifts. But perhaps the best part of the museum was the rear knot garden; an idyllic walled haven of flowers and leaves woven into a pretty green box parterre. You can buy lunch in the café and eat it here, or—like the cabbie and I did—munch on your own DIY picnic fare in the shade. Note that the Garden Museum is currently undergoing an enormous redevelopment and expansion program, and should be open again in early 2017. It will contain the country's first Archive of Garden Design, preserving the letters, designs, photographs and personal artefacts of our great makers of gardens. There will also be an improved schedule of garden exhibitions, following on from the already-successful displays in the past, including *Fashion and Gardens* and the Russell Page exhibition in 2015.

Lambeth Palace Road, London. www.gardenmuseum.org.uk

98

GEFFRYE MUSEUM A little-known museum in London's East End, the Geffrye is also known as the 'Museum of the Home'. It explores English houses from 1600 to the present day, focusing on the living rooms of London's influential and ever-changing middle and upper classes. It's set behind a grand garden but it also features it own large but charming garden at the rear, which is divided into garden designs of various periods in time: Victorian, Edwardian and so on. It's difficult to know which is more interesting in this museum: the gardens or the interior design exhibitions. Both are surprisingly enlightening. The garden perhaps nudges ahead, if only because the various garden 'rooms' are such lovely spaces to be on a spring or summer day, learning about the exotics adored by the Victorians, the herb gardens favoured in the medieval era (the herb garden here is glorious) and of course the Edwardian borders. The key is to read all the small signs and plaques, both outside and inside the museum; they're where the interesting bits are hidden. One large board, that was almost lost behind a door, showed in fascinating detail how gardens became popular with the upper-middle class. Even the small signs in the medieval herb garden are enthralling.

136 Kingsland Road, Hoxton, London. www.geffrye-museum.org.uk

This page clockwise from top left *Verdant plantings at Geffrye Museum medieval garden; walled entry into the garden; museum interior; garden education details*
Opposite *The Geffrye Museum's glorious herb garden*

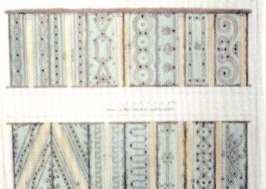

Top
Back Garden at Mr Paul Sandby's House, 4 St. George's Row, Tyburn, c1773, watercolour and bodycolour, by Paul Sandby

The artist's very formal garden, on the right, is probably less typical than that of his neighbours, which is filled with plants, flowers and activity. The lively scene, with ladies hoeing, raking and watering, gives the impression that this garden was a place of relaxed informality.
© Copyright the Trustees of The British Museum

Above left
The garden at 14 St. James's Square, Bristol (detail), c1805 Watercolour, attributed to Thomas Pole

This painting shows the late-eighteenth century preference in town gardens for neat and tidy beds, here filled with mainly small, brightly coloured plants, spaced apart so that the soil between is visible. Some of these may be fashionable 'florists' flowers', plants grown solely for their decorative qualities. They included carnation, tulip, anemone, ranunculus, hyacinth, polyanthus, pink and auricula.
Bristol City Museum and Art Gallery

Left
'Fourteen Designs for small town gardens', from *Hints on the Formation of Gardens and Pleasure Grounds*, 1812, by John Claudius Loudon

J. C. Loudon's published designs were suitable for the typically long, narrow gardens found behind terraced houses in London. The

100   **HAMPSTEAD HILL GARDEN AND PERGOLA** This is a rather eerie but utterly romantic corner of London that few people discover as they traipse around this popular idyll of a village. It's a little slice of faded grandeur on the West Heath that was built by Lord Leverhulme at the start of the century as a setting for his extravagant soirees. There are impressive gardens but the most dramatic part is an elevated walkway and formal pergola planed with entwining vines that now create the most enchanting canopy. It's a glimpse of Edwardian times where the rich did as they please, and usually very tastefully. The best time to visit is in the afternoon, when the light slants aross the colums and a kind of painterly atmosphere settles on the scene.

Inverforth Close, Hampstead, London.

KENSINGTON GARDENS, SUNKEN GARDENS AND ORANGERY
Kensington Palace began life in 1605 but it was not until it was bought by William III in 1689 that it became a royal palace, with a Baroque parterre garden, vegetable gardens, orchards, an orangery (added in 1704), and a private road (Rotton Row) to Hyde Park Corner. It was also linked to a Baroque network of avenues in Kensington Garden. Centuries later, however, only faint lines of the old gardens survive. But there is one secret garden that still stands: an exquisite sunken garden that was built over the old part of the royal estate given over to potting sheds. It draws upon the classical proportions of the old Baroque gardens but is much simpler in design, yet no less enchanting. The garden surrounds an ornamental pond that features fountains formed from reused 18th-century water cisterns (retrieved from the nearby palace). Extending out from these fountains are terraces flecked with paving and ornamental flower beds. In the spring, tulips, wallflowers and pansies bloom, while in the summer, geraniums, cannas and begonias offer colour. Surrounding the garden is an arched arbour of red-twigged lime, with viewpoints spaced along the sides, so visitors can 'peek' into the garden. In the summer, this shady tunnel provides the perfect place to view either the Sunken Garden to the north or the re-landscaped gardens to the south. The Orangery to the north of the gardens is a charming place to have a cup of tea afterwards. It was built in 1704 as an elaborate greenhouse to protect Queen Anne's citrus trees from the harsh frosts of winter. She soon realised that the Orangery's graceful architecture made it a perfect venue for fashionable court entertaining away from the chaos of 'town'. For most of the 18th century, the gardens were closed to the public except on Saturdays, and only to the 'respectably dressed'.

Kensington Gardens, Kensington, London.

ROYAL BOTANIC GARDENS, KEW Everyone knows about Kew's world-famous Royal Botanic Gardens, a UNESCO World Heritage site, but what isn't as well known are the horticultural gems that are tucked into the edges of this wondrous green space. Right in the far corner of Kew is the charming hideaway known as Queen Charlotte's Cottage, which served as a private haven for Queen Charlotte and her friends in the 18th century, primarily for resting or taking tea after walks in the gardens. It's an early example of a cottage orné, a rustic cottage built as a country retreat, but not as a residence. Near the cottage was a field in which exotic animals were kept, including kangaroos, and you can still glimpse oriental cattle and colourful Tartarian pheasants wandering about, which are all that remain from those eccentric days.

Kew Palace is another lovely place that's well worth visiting. One of the best resources about it is its own People's Library, a marvellous source of all sorts of fascinating information. There are documents containing 18th- and early-19th-century accounts for the house, and excerpts from the diaries of men and women acquainted with George III and his family, as well as information on the family itself. But perhaps the most interesting resource is a video that tells you about the fabric of the house, and about its refurbishment throughout the ages. Oh, and the extraordinary Victorian Palm House is a must-see while you're here. Venture up the ornate iron stairs to the mezzanine above and inhale the scent of paradise.

Kew, Richmond, Surrey, TW9. www.kew.org

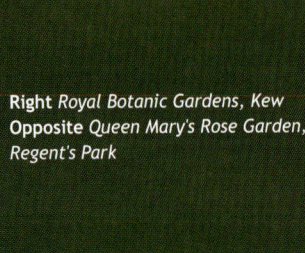

Right *Royal Botanic Gardens, Kew*
Opposite *Queen Mary's Rose Garden, Regent's Park*

QUEEN MARY'S ROSE GARDEN, REGENT'S PARK Few people realise that the largest rose garden in England is right in the middle of London. This is an extraordinary place; a real horticultural oasis just steps from the West End. It's named after Queen Mary, the wife of King George V, and features more than 12,000 roses set over various gardens, from lovely long avenues to a formal parterre to nooks and crannies with seats to relax in. It's tricky to find—shrubberies are strategically designed and located to add a sense of mystery and privacy to the gardens—but oh, what a sight when you do stumble upon the first of the extensive rose beds! Examples of most rose varieties are included in the scented mix, from the classics to the most modern English roses. It is a blissfully quiet and peaceful sanctuary in the middle of one of the busiest cities in the world. Even in May, before the roses are in bloom, the perfume is intoxicating. There is also a delphinium garden and a begonia garden, with 9000 begonias. To see the best blooms, visit in the first two weeks of June.

Regent's Park, London. www.royalparks.org.uk

PETERSHAM NURSERIES The delightful Petersham Nurseries is fairly well known, as much for its charming setting—in a series of pretty greenhouses in Richmond—and its covetable garden goods as for its unusual restaurant, which received a Michelin star under previous chef Skye Gyngell. Garden lovers flock here for the cute wellies, the charming homewares, the pretty pot plants and the idyllic views across the meadows to the Thames (from outside the front gate). However, what isn't as well known is the fact that the nursery offers fantastic horticultural classes in its newly launched School of Garden. Subjects include many of the things that the nursery is celebrated for, including cutting gardens, scented gardens, potting and growing bulbs, and pruning, but there are short half-day courses, including the Ultimate Cutting Garden workshop. All include lunch as well as seed trays and flowers to take home—and all for only £15. So incredibly cheap!

Church Lane, Petersham Road, Richmond, London.

www.petershamnurseries.com/events

ST DUNSTAN IN THE EAST RUINED CHURCH GARDEN What a magical place this is! If gardens can be a spiritual experience, this is certainly one place to feel at peace. After this fine church was severely damaged in the Blitz of 1941—although thankfully Wren's tower and steeple survived the blast— the Anglican Church decided not to rebuild it. Instead, in 1967, the City of London decided to turn the ruins into an unusual public garden, which opened in 1970. Since then, the plants have slowly blanketed the old church walls, winding their way through windows and around doors to create an eerie but also enchanting picture of Mother Nature meeting God. It's a lovely place to escape the crowds and traffic of London. There are many seats inside the church walls, which are gorgeous for a mini picnic on a sunny day.

St Dunstan's Hill, City of London, London.

Above and opposite *Petersham Nurseries*

WILD AT HEART Florist Nikki Tibble has gained an international reputation for astonishingly glamorous bouquets and equally eye-catching stores. In fact, she is arguably one of the top florists working in the world today. Fans flock to her shops just to see the merchandising—although the flowers come a close second. The most popular of her stores is the one in Pimlico Road, which is festooned with roses, peonies, delphiniums, hydrangeas, sweet peas and other petals during Chelsea Flower Show week each year (it really is spectacular), but she started at her (smaller) Notting Hill location in 1993. It was there that she put in a claim for the lease on a tiny space at the newly designed 'Turquoise Island', a quaint building designed by celebrated architect Piers Gough that hid a public loo on one side. She beat 70 rivals to the lease and her

new business was born. It has remained solid ever since. However, now she spends less time arranging bouquets and more time doing events all around the world. Still, her staff are brilliant, and any of her shops is worth a visit for the colour, creativity and sheer exuberance. As well as the Notting Hill and Belgravia locations, there is also a small Wild at Heart outpost in the entrance of the Liberty London store on Great Marlborough Street.

222 Westbourne Grove, Notting Hill, and 30A Pimlico Road, Belgravia, London. www.wildatheart.com

Above *Wild at Heart in Belgravia*
Opposite *Wild at Heart in Notting Hill*

MUSEUMS AND HISTORIC HOUSES
(SPECIALISING IN DESIGN)

18 STAFFORD TERRACE (LINLEY SAMBOURNE HOUSE) Tucked away off Kensington High Street, this enthralling place is often missed by tourists, partly because not many know about it and partly because until recently it's been difficult to book a place on a tour in advance. (This has now changed.) However, this is a good thing: it means visitors are able to see this intriguing house without throngs elbowing each other behind velvet ropes. It's a timewarp of an interior that looks just as it did in the year 1900, still one of the most glamorous years in history. In fact, stepping through the doors is like stepping into Miss Haversham's mansion. The interior has been left largely untouched since owner, *Punch* cartoonist Edward Linley Sambourne and his family lived herd until 1910. (The generations of owners also kept the interior as it was; they, too, must have known how beautiful and precious it was and how important it was to preserve.) It's a snapshot of middle-class Aestheticism, from the elegant wallpaper and hundreds of beautifully framed prints, to the collections of silver. It almost looks like a spread in *World of Interiors* magazine. A gorgeous, gorgeous place, and a must-see for design and decorating professionals who like to walk (and work) on the traditional side.

18 Stafford Terrace, Kensington, London.

575 WANDSWORTH ROAD This enchanting place—part gingerbread house, part Brothers Grimm storybook—is not a museum as such, but it certainly displays a wondrous dedication to design. And how it has remained one of London's best-kept secrets is as much of a mystery as the house itself. The National Trust certainly doesn't market it; it doesn't

need to: tours are booked up months in advance. To make things more difficult, only six people are allowed on each tour, and there are only a few tours each week, and only at certain times of the year. So, yes, you have to be determined. But design lovers, and particularly craftspeople, *should* be tenacious, because 575 is one of the most ingenious, most beautiful, most extraordinary cottages in all of London. It was the home of Kenyan poet and civil servant Khadambi Asalache, who lived here until his death in 2006. Khadambi Asalache's life is the stuff of a VS Naipaul story. Born in 1935, he grew up in rural Kenya as the son of a Maasai, where he read Shakespeare while herding cattle, and longed for an artistic life. Following his dreams, he moved to Rome to study art and architecture at university, and then travelled to London in 1960, where he attempted to be a poet and writer. To supplement his income, he worked for the BBC African Service before joining the Treasury. In 1981, he bought a humble, two-up two-down Georgian terraced house at 575 Wandsworth Road, for no other reason than its proximity to a bus stop that took him straight into Whitehall. Having been occupied by squatters, it was derelict, and a bargain price. It was also affected by damp from the laundromat next door, which he tried to fix, with little success. The damp parts that he couldn't restore were an eyesore. As a house, it was so ugly to his poet's eye and heart that he felt impelled to turn it into a place of extraordinary beauty. He began with books, pictures and furnishings, including magnificent porcelain collections, that were a reflection of his wide range of classical interests, but they weren't enough. So he began carving. Using a simple pocket knife and salvaged timber offcuts he found in nearby skips and building yards, he spent his evenings and weekends single-handedly

covering all the walls with an intricate reticulated fretwork. Sometimes he worked at his kitchen table for 12 hours or more, carving the panels. It took him 20 years. And a few worn-out pocket knives. But in the end, the house was a little bit of magic. Every wall and most of the ceilings featured intricate illustrations of African animals, people, botany, life, landscapes and stories. Even the staircase featured fretwork. It is so beautiful that at certain times of the day, usually in summer when the sun sets later, the light streaming through the fretwork shutters over the front windows turns the space into an almost spiritual experience, as if you're in a mosque when the light shimmers through the windows. Khadambi Asalache never said much about his creation while he was alive—an intensely private man, he only shared his home with friends, colleagues and his partner—but he did acquiesce that he had taken inspiration from the Great Mosque of Cordoba, the Alhambra and Generalife in Granada, doors in Zanzibar, panelled interiors in Damascus, and the waterside houses of Istanbul. There are also touches of Rococo, and indeed British bohemianism! After the property was restored by the National Trust, it was highlighted in the highly regarded magazine *World of Interiors* (July / August 1990), and then subsequent magazines, including the *Sunday Telegraph Magazine* in February 2000 and more recently in *House and Garden* in 2015. Tim Knox, director of Sir John Soane's Museum, described it as an "extremely serious and carefully worked out exercise in horror vacui, taking its inspiration from the Mozarabic reticulations of the Moorish kingdoms of Granada". The National Trust is still determining how to show it to the public, as the rooms are so narrow and the fretwork so fragile, that only a certain number of people (usually six) can go through the house at once time. However, the Trust acknowledges that it's a "great work of art and an important part of our built heritage". This is indeed one of London's true design treasures: a thing of wonder. The fretwork may be rustic and on the amateurish side, but the affect it creates is as beautiful and as admirable as the profoundly civilised and educated gentleman who made it. A must-see for artists and designers, no matter what material you work in. It will show you the value of tenacity.

575 Wandsworth Road, Lambeth, London.

www.nationaltrust.org.uk/575-wandsworth-road

BLYTHE HOUSE Originally built as the headquarters of the Post Office Savings Bank, this enormous old building is now used to store the archives of the Victoria and Albert, Science and British Museums. The V&A part of it is known as the Clothworkers' Centre, and there are guided tours that take place on the last Friday of the month. Places are limited so you need to book in advance, but if you're interested in fashion, textiles or design, these fashion archives offer an amazing experience. The main storage space is floor the size of football field that's set up with state-of-the-art cabinets, which roll back and forth in futuristic fashion. It's all very high-tech. But it has to be because inside these enormous silver 'vaults' are thousands of vintage fashion pieces—more than 50,000 in total. Chanel. Balenciaga. Givenchy. Dior. There are so many, your jaw will drop as you walk past all the labels on the end of the cabinets. The curator will also choose a few items to pull out, so you can examine the Queen's favourite gown, or an original cream jacket and black skirt from Dior's 'New Look' collection. It's fascinating to see such pieces up close. The detail that goes into such couture is extraordinary. The V&A has always been held in high regard by fashion and textile lovers, but the team in this quiet corner of West Kensington should be applauded for their dedication to preserving such magnificent history.

Tours available by emailing clothworkers@vam.ac.uk.

23 Blythe Road, London.

(Note: Blythe House, the building that these archives are stored in, has recently been sold, and the V&A is considering new premises. Look up the Clothworkers' Centre on the V&A's website for updates on a new venue.)

From opposite left to right *Exterior at William Morris; the Queen's Gallery; a photographic exhibition on Avedon at the V&A (one of the best design museums in the world); Blythe House*

DENNIS SEVERS HOUSE If you've 'done' all the major sights and museums, and you or your kids want something different, take them here. It's a wonderfully eccentric place groaning with atmosphere—something between a museum and a film set—that will capture the imaginations of young and old alike. It's the concept of former Californian Dennis Severs, who came to London and made his home in this Spitalfields merchant's house, before deciding it would perhaps look better if it were returned to its original state. He felt it was the home of a family of Huguenot weavers and so he set about restoring it, just as it would have been had they left one evening for a ball and never returned. Everything is preserved just so, from the plates on the tables to the half-burned candles. The best time to see it is during an evening tour, when the house is lit by those candles and the shadows make the rooms even more authentic. Guides encourage guests to remain silent, so they can properly hear, see and smell what life was like centuries ago. As the guides says: "Being in this house is almost like walking through a painting." Some people say the place is haunted. It certainly feels that way. But it's also mysterious and magical and utterly memorable. Kids will love it. The house is hidden away on a cobbled street near Liverpool Street station, and open sporadically, so check the website and tour times for details.

18 Folgate Street, Spitalfields. London. www.dennissevershouse.co.uk

DESIGN MUSEUM Some people visit the Design Museum just to shop for lavish coffee-table titles at the bookshop and dine at one of the two cafés. It's a great place to meet friends for these reasons. But of course you couldn't visit without wandering through the exhibitions. Opened in 1989 following its original incarnation as the Boilerhouse established by Terence Conran, the Design Museum encompasses modern and contemporary industrial and fashion design, graphics, architecture and multimedia. It used to be on the other side of town at an interesting but perhaps out-of-the-way location near Shad Thames. Its new location in the formerly derelict Commonwealth Institute in Holland Park, off High Street Kensington, will likely see a lot more tourists visiting it, due to the fact that there are many other design venues nearby (including Blythe House). Both the architecture and the exhibits, including the permanent and constantly changing displays, are causing much fuss and excitement with the media, so let's hope it draws the crowds that this design museum deserves.

224–238 Kensington High Street, Kensington, London. www.designmuseum.org

EMERY WALKER TRUST The Emery Walker Trust, which is also known as 7 Hammersmith Terrace (its address) is described by its trustees as the 'last surviving Arts and Crafts interior in Britain'. While I'm not sure that's quite true, it's certainly a fairly extensive and intact one, with few signs of modern life, furniture, fittings or indeed technology.

(Definitely no MacBooks in the corners here!) The house is part of a terrace of 17 tall, narrow houses, built between Chiswick Mall and Lower Mall, Hammersmith, on the north bank of the River Thames in the 1750s, when this area was mostly fields and rural views. This scenery continued right through until the late 1870s, when the character began changing considerably as waterworks, breweries, timber wharves and other industries sprang up along the river. Despite the development, families still loved the riverside location, and even today, there are vistas across the Thames that are nothing but trees. Those who moved into this terrace included Emery Walker, who owned this house, the bookbinder TJ Cobden-Sanderson, with whom Emery Walker set up the Doves Press in 1900, the calligrapher Edward Johnston, and the art critic FG Stephens. Walker's friend William Morris was a short distance away in Upper Mall, and it was he who really influenced the interior of this residence: the rooms are a tribute to William Morris's designs. The halls are wallpapered in Morris; the living room is a deeply atmospheric room with deep blue-green Morris wallpaper; the dining room (more pale blue Morris wallpaper) features a number of mementoes gifted by William Morris himself, and a 17th-century chair from his library, given to Walker after Morris's death by his widow, Janey; and the upstairs bedroom features original Daisy wallpaper, Morris & Co. chairs, a 1920s four-poster and an exquisite bedcover worked by May Morris in crewelwork, which is a match for that on William Morris's bed at Kelmscott Manor. The simple but pretty walled garden leads right down to the wall embanking the river and is laid out as it was in Sir Emery's time. Among the plants are an ancient jasmine and roses, and a lovely wisteria. The house is currently closed for extensive renovations but will open again in early 2017.

7 Hammersmith Terrace, Hammersmith, London. www.emerywalker.org

FASHION AND TEXTILE MUSEUM This museum is small but some of its exhibitions are well curated. Founded by legendary fashion designer Zandra Rhodes and operated by Newham College, it has a constantly evolving display of things relating to fashion, textiles and jewellery. The gift shop is worth a browse, too; it stocks a carefully selected range of products from talented designers to those who are making a name for themselves.

83 Bermondsey Street, Bermondsey Village, London. www.ftmlondon.org

Opposite *Exterior plaque at the Emery Walker Trust*
Above left *One of the Fashion and Textile Museum's exhibitons was Riviera Style, which showed a glamorous collection of clothing and accessories worn by the sea. It included an iconic Chanel outfit with accompanying beret, cute retro bathing outfits from the 1950s, striped Breton tops, palazzo pants, and romantic old posters.*
Above right *Fashion and Textile Museum*

FENTON HOUSE The glorious gardens that surround this 17th-century merchant's house are wonderful on a summer's day. There's even a nice orchard and a lovely walled kitchen garden. But it's inside where the heart really starts to race with envy: enormous collections of paintings, porcelain, needlework and instruments fill every room. Time your visit to coincide with one of the lunchtime or evening concerts to hear these being played.

Hampstead Grove, Hampstead, London. www.nationaltrust.org.uk

HAM HOUSE This lavishly decorated 17th-century house has for years been one of those places you hear about and think: hmm, sounds a bit dull. Well, it's actually not dull at all. There are lots of enlightening corners, walls, furnishings and fittings. For example, who knew that picture framing changed dramatically in the 1620s and 1630s as a result of the collecting activities of King Charles I, from simple designs to elaborately carved and gilt frames? And who knew the Stuarts were so into bathing rituals, as evidenced by one of the oldest purpose-built 17th-century spa-style bathrooms in England, right here in the house. But the real surprises come in two unexpected places: the gorgeous garden (especially the famous lavender and santolina parterre and walled kitchen garden) and the recently renovated below-stairs area, with its grand kitchen. There's much to see and learn here. It's also one of the most haunted houses in Britain, with the Duchess of Lauderdale and her dog the subject of numerous sightings through the years. Look out for her. All in all, utterly fascinating.

Ham Street, Richmond-upon-Thames.

www.nationaltrust.org.uk/ham-house-and-garden

HOGARTH'S HOUSE In the year 1749, Hogarth and his family took over the lease on a pretty, three-storey house with a large garden and orchard on the western edge of Chiswick Town, where London turned to fields and pastoral pleasures. It was to be their country retreat, far from the noise of Leicester Fields (now Leicester Square). Several of Hogarth's friends already lived nearby, including antiquarian Thomas Morrell, and American political writer and dramatist James Ralph. The Hogarths embraced country life. They adored the fruit trees and nut walk in their new walled garden, and Hogarth established a 'painting room' at the bottom of the estate, which he used right up until a few days before his death. After he passed, his widow Jane kept the house and ran the print-selling business. The family adored the area, but the relished the house most of all, and it's easy to see why. It's serene and peaceful and imbued with a light that inspires and delights. Interestingly, the interior still looks like stylish houses you'd find today in Scandinavia or chic interior magazines, with pared-back painted walls and sun flooding through windows. If only we could all live in such an idyll. As you'd expect, there's a wonderful collection of his prints, many of them framed in the narrow, black-and-gold frames that are now called Hogarth frames, in his honour. If you don't know much about Hogarth, this is a beautiful place to start.

Hogarth Lane, Great West Road, London.

www.williamhogarthtrust.org.uk

KEATS' HOUSE If you saw director Jane Campion's beautiful and moving film *Bright Star* about the three-year romance between 19th-century poet John Keats and Fanny Brawne near the end of Keats' life, you'll know how gorgeous his home in Hampstead was. This gracious 19th-century house was only home to the famous poet for 17 months, but it was close to his heart, mostly because he lost his heart here, to the lovely Miss Brawne. Wandering around, it feels as though he's just left for his ill-fated trip to Rome, and there'll be a postcard in the letterbox any day now. But of course that's not the case, and so there's a tinge of sadness too, especially for what Fanny must have endured when she was told the news of his untimely death. (She cut her hair, wore black and walked the Heath for three weeks, in deep mourning.) The interiors have been faithfully restored to the quality they were in the 19th century and the garden where he composed 'Ode to a Nightingale' and exchanged tender kisses with his young love is still there too, and just as beautiful—and surprisingly moving on a summer's day. You can almost imagine the two lovers are still here, somewhere in some quiet corner, oblivious to the world around them. If you haven't read Keats, then watch Jane Campion's film. Watch it and weep. Then come here and pay tribute.

Keats Grove, Hampstead, London. cityoflondon.gov.uk

MARIANNE NORTH GALLERY AT KEW If you love art and horticulture in equal measure, this is the place for you. It's a gallery of incredibly beautiful botanical paintings made during the 19th century by artist Marianne North as she travelled the globe. There are more than 800 paintings of flowers, landscapes, animals and birds, from regions afar as Jamaica, Brazil, Sarawak, Java, Sri Lanka, the Seychelles and Chile. It's one of the two permanent galleries of botanical art at Kew Gardens. The other is the Shirley Sherwood Gallery of Botanical Art, the first in the world dedicated solely to botanical art. Both are marvellous, uplifting odes to flowers, paint and nature.

Kew, Richmond, Surrey. www.kew.org

NEW LONDON ARCHITECTURE The awkwardly titled New London Architecture concerns itself with all issues related to London-based architecture, planning, development and construction. It's of interest to architects, naturally, but it's also curiously interesting to those of us who love London's skyline. There are publicly accessible galleries that seek to inform and educate us about the capital's rapidly changing cityscape, and an ongoing program of debates and discussions about various architecture and urban issues. There are also architecture walks, which are great on a sunny day. But if you only have time for a quick visit, be sure to check out the giant scale model of central London. Measuring 12 metres, the 1:1500 scale model also includes proposed London buildings that have secured planning permission and are in development.

26 Store Street, Holborn, London. www.newlondonarchitecture.org

OSTERLEY PARK The Georgian 'look' has come back into interior design and decorating recently. In fact, pale pink and pale blue were the Pantone colours of 2016, although Pantone has given them the modern names of 'Rose Quartz' and 'Serenity', which sound rather pretentious. If you want to see the original Georgian style in all its understated glamour, head here, to Osterley Park, a grand Georgian estate on the outskirts of the city. Originally built in 1575 and transformed by Robert Adam into an exquisite 18th-century, neo-classical villa, the superb rooms contain some of the country's best examples of Adam's work. Everything here is going to make you sigh with pleasure, from the elegant colour schemes to the lovely Georgian furniture. Don't miss the astonishingly decorated Etruscan Dressing Room, inspired by the illustrated work 'Antiquités etrusques, grecques et romaines', which was painted by the artist Pietro Maria Borgnis. The elegant library is also an understated space that looks surprisingly modern. It has the same ornate decorative plaster ceilings and stucco work wall panels as found elsewhere in the house, but has been painted in a soft white, which shows up not only the books but also the delicate curves of the polished wood furniture.

Jersey Road, Isleworth, Middlesex. nationaltrust.org.uk

PITZHANGER MANOR Although it's still being renovated and isn't set to open until 2018, it's still worth including this marvellous Regency villa that was Sir John Soane's former home, because it's an extraordinary building and all the updates about the amazing interior and its restoration work show it's set to be as intriguing as Soane's Museum (see page 114). Soane lived here from 1800–1810, when the area was more pastoral, and later described it as his 'dream home'. He used it to entertain friends and clients, including the painter JMW Turner, who lived around the corner at

Sandycomb Lodge (also the focus of restoration efforts). The £11 million funds that are going into the upgrade of Pitzhanger Manor will restore the Grade I–listed house completely, creating a major arts and heritage site that tells the story of Soane's life. Details will be released closer to opening.

http://www.pitzhanger.org.uk

QUEEN'S GALLERY I only discovered this lovely place when I attended the small but extraordinary exhibition 'Painting Paradise: The Art of the Garden' here in 2015. It was beautifully staged against the gallery's enormous rooms and high walls, with the bright green colours of the garden paintings set magnificently against the rose-red walls. Until then, I hadn't realised the Queen had her own gallery at Buckingham Palace, much less her own personal and extension collection of 'garden art'. The gallery is at the west front of the Palace, on the site of a chapel bombed during the Second World War. In 2001, it was renovated for modern exhibitions, and modern audiences, and reopened on 21 May 2002 by Elizabeth II to coincide with her Golden Jubilee. The extension added the current Doric columns to the entrance portico and several new rooms, more than tripling the size of the building. It now exhibits works of art from the Royal Collection (those works owned by the King or Queen "in trust for the nation" rather than privately) on a rotating basis. See what's on here next time you're in London; you will be pleasantly surprised.

Buckingham Palace, Buckingham Palace Road, London.

www.royalcollection.org.uk

SANDYCOMB LODGE Most of us have heard of the great landscape artist JMW Turner, but what isn't as well known is where he lived and painted. Well, this tranquil setting was his retreat from the world; a place where he found inspiration, and landscapes to study and paint. He discovered it in 1805, when he was leading a highly pressured life, both professionally and personally. In need of peace, he rented a house close to the Thames in Isleworth, and soon after bought his own plot of land, with dreams of creating a country refuge. He longed for a country villa in Italianate style, which would be suitable for him, as a single man, and his elderly father as companion and housekeeper. Having built it, he spent many happy days here, sketching, fishing, entertaining, and of course, painting. Today, the house is undergoing restoration work, but will reopen in the summer of 2017. Keep an eye on the website for updates: this is bound to be a hidden museum gem in the making.

Sandycombe Lodge, 40 Sandycombe Road, Twickenham.

www.turnerintwickenham.org.uk

SOANE'S MUSEUM Sir John Soane's Museum is the former London home of the neo-classical architect (1753–1837). It consists of three townhouses, which he knocked together, and was bequeathed to the nation as a museum of architecture, though it is more like a cabinet of curiosities acquired during Soane's travels. One *Guardian* journalist called it "a crazy labyrinth of art, architecture and history—poetry in three dimensions". It's an apt description because the paintings, drawing, sculpture and antiquities are not arranged in any particular method but rather in a more 'ad hoc' way, following the way that Soane himself placed objects here and there as he carved out more spaces to display his ever-growing collections. It's a wondrous museum over many levels, with the feel of a private home that once belonging to an extraordinary and slightly eccentric collector—which is, of course, what it is.

13 Lincoln's Inn Fields, London. www.soane.org

SOMERSET HOUSE Since it was reinvigorated a few years ago, this superb neo-classical building overlooking the Thames has been putting on some amazing exhibitions. Originally the site of a Tudor palace, it was extended over the centuries, and largely forgotten about (it was used for offices and societies) until it was resurrected in the late 20th century as a centre for the visual arts. There is now a constantly changing, year-round program of major arts and cultural events at this historic site, including large-scale contemporary exhibitions. Tim Walker's *Storyteller* exhibition in the East Wing was one of the most beautiful photographic exhibitions ever staged in London, while the fashion exhibition *Valentino: Master of Couture* was a mammoth show that brought international fans from far and wide. There is also a small Rizzoli bookshop here selling art, design, architecture, interior and photographic titles, not just by Rizzoli but many different publishers.

Strand, London. www.somersethouse.org.uk

THE NEW TATE MODERN When the new Tate Modern opened in 2000, it caused a huge stir in both the media and the public for its extraordinary architecture and its bold, ambitious exhibitions. Almost two decades later, the new Tate Modern, which opened in June 2016, is doing exactly the same. Its astounding, pyramid-like building, which stretches 10 storeys on top of The Tanks, features a height that replicates that of the chimney of the existing Tate Modern building, which was originally designed as a power station by Giles Gilbert Scott in the 1950s. Inside, the interior is designed to display a greater variety of artworks and artists, and will be the world's first gallery spaces dedicated to live art, film and installations. There is also a spectacular new roof terrace with 360-degree views of the River Thames, St Paul's Cathedral and the dramatic London skyline.

Bankside, London. www.tate.org.uk

V&A'S SECRET GALLERIES AND DISPLAYS The V&A is renowned the world over for its many superb design galleries, so I won't go into detail on the more well-known ones here. What I want to do is highlight the lesser-known displays, which are hidden upstairs and in corners that visitors don't normally venture into. The first is the beautiful, mesmerising piece known as the Stoke Edith Hanging. This is a room-sized work of embroidery on linen, canvas, silk and wool that was done by the staff of Stoke Edith Hall in Herefordshire from 1710 to 1720. It is difficult to articulate how magnificent it is. To consider the size of it is one thing; to consider how long it must have taken to embroider is quite another. It depicts a scene of a formal garden, laid out in late-17th-century Anglo-Dutch style. The detail is incredible. Even the shadows of the topiary have been embroidered into place. Such hangings would have originally been used like woven tapestries, to line the walls of a room with decorative, narrative scenes. It was gifted to the government in lieu of tax and allocated to the V&A in 1996, and it almost seems as if the

V&A doesn't know what to do with it. Perhaps the V&A needs a separate garden wing for such horticultural fancies and follies? (Located in the British Galleries, room 54b, case WE.) An even larger display of intricate craftsmanship is the Norfolk House Music Room, a rather ordinary title for an extraordinary room. This is one of the most spectacular and yet least-known parts of the V&A. It's a grand, gilded ballroom (originally a music room) that was salvaged from Norfolk House in St James's Square in the 1930s. Norfolk House was the London residence of the Dukes of Norfolk until 1938, until the land, which was recognised as being more valuable than the house, was sold and the house demolished. Thankfully someone had the good sense to save this room, which has now been reconstructed in the west wing of the V&A. You can see the French influence in the design of it: it does look very Versailles-ish. Even ol' Horace Walpole was impressed when he encountered it in its original setting. (There's more about the details of the embellishments and decorative fantasies on the V&A's extensive website. Just type Norfolk House Music Room into the search tool.) It's a wonderful reminder of London's lost palaces, and a distant, elegant age. Finally, in a quiet gallery on the south side, there is a display detailing that grandest of grand exhibitions, the Great Exhibition in 1851. This is pertinent because many of the objects in the exhibition were used as the first collection for the South Kensington Museum, which opened in 1857 and eventually became the Victoria and Albert Museum (V&A). The Great Exhibition was the first international exhibition of manufactured products and was enormously influential on the development of many aspects of society, including art and design education, international trade and relations, and even tourism. It was organised by Henry Cole and Prince Albert, and held in the purpose-built Crystal Palace in Hyde Park designed by Joseph Paxton, who had been building greenhouses for the Duke of Devonshire

at Chatsworth. Paxton proposed a gigantic prefabricated building of iron and glass, which used 300,000 sheets in the largest size ever made. Steam engines on-site drove the machinery to cut the wooden glazing bars as well as the 40 kilometres (24 miles) of Paxton's patent guttering used to hold the glass in position. It took less than nine months to complete, and when it was finished, the enormous structure was capable of holding more than 100,000 objects, from hairpins to steam hammers, half from Britain and the Empire, half from other countries. Queen Victoria loved it! There are various pieces illustrating and detailing the Great Exhibition, but perhaps the most interesting is the original catalogue, a two-part publication done in two enormous red-covered books. Honestly, you could read about this gorgeous, gargantuan exhibition for hours! While you're wandering around the V&A, don't miss the Fashion Gallery, which was renovated a few years ago and still looks fresh and modern. It's a beautiful, inspirational, memorable, utterly joyous exhibition of frocks, shoes, ballgowns, day dresses and other sartorial finery from the late 17th century to the turn of the century. And it's completely free. How often can you say that about fashion today?

Cromwell Road, South Kensington, London. www.vam.ac.uk

Opposite *Soane's Museum façade; Tim Walker's exhibition at Somerset House*
This page left to right *Somerset House courtyard; V&A exhibition detail*

WILLIAM MORRIS GALLERY Most designers and decorators know of William Morris and his work. He was not only a 19th-century textile designer, craftsman, writer, conservationist and socialist, but also one of the major leaders of the Arts and Crafts movement, which helped popularise decorative arts. This large Grade II–listed Georgian residence was his family's home from 1848 to 1856. Morris lived here with his widowed mother and his eight brothers and sisters from the age of 14 until he was 22. The young Morrises used the garden moat for boating and fishing in summer and for ice-skating in winter. In tribute to Morris's remarkable talents, it has been converted into a museum paying homage to his work. There are floral wallpapers, woodblock prints, and tiles, as well as the designs done by his friends and collaborators. Following a renovation and relaunch in 2012, the museum won Britain's prestigious Museum of the Year Award. It's a bit of a trek to get to, but if you're a Morris fan, it's definitely worth a look. There's also the William Morris Society in Hammersmith, located in a small downstairs part of Morris's former home, Kelmscott House. It's not extensive, only a few rooms, but it does show many of his patterns and designs.

William Morris Gallery: Lloyd Park, Lloyd Park, Forest Road, Walthamstow, London. www.wmgallery.org.uk; William Morris Society: 26 Upper Mall, Hammersmith, London. www.williammorrissociety.org

Above *The rose-covered entrance to the William Morris Society in Chiswick, one of two Morris-dedicated museums in London*
Opposite *A William Morris wallpaper design, seen inside the William Morris Society, which is set inside his former home in Chiswick, 'Kelmscott House'*

118

BOOKSHOPS

ASSOULINE (MAISON ASSOULINE) Bookstores are as different as the books they sell. Some are quiet, dignified spaces that smell of old leather, aged paper, well-trodden oak floors and the reassuring aroma of books that have stood the test of time and look even better in their old age. Others are whimsical, colourful, enticing places, where book jackets vie for attention like kids at a party: pick me, pick me. And then there are the bookstores that are more like museums or galleries, where books are as revered as works of art, and displayed as such. This is the case with Maison Assouline; one of the most striking bookstores in all of London. Now it has to be said that, unlike its closest competitor, Rizzoli bookstore (owned by the international publishing house), Assouline only sells its own Assouline titles. But wander in anyway: you'll be dazed by the building. It's an incredibly grand, converted bank designed by Sir Edwin Lutyens in 1922, and is in the middle of the moneyed neighbourhood of Mayfair, traditionally the browsing ground for serious bibliofiles searching for signed first editions, antiquarian titles, and long-lost books on, say, maps of the 1800s. Assouline has none of those. Instead, it has books on Valentino, high-heeled shoes, and the French Riviera. Oversized, glossy, glamorous numbers in clamshells and slipcases. Books that cost more than you want to spend. In one year. (One magazine article called it "posh publishing".) While the Mondrian-esque bookshelves and their contents are beautiful, it's the overall space that really deserves to be gazed at. The double-height room soars skyward, anchored at the end by a handsome timber staircase that rises, firstly, to a mezzanine of leathery loveliness that shows how bespoke bindery is done, and then to rooms full of furniture and whimsy. This is Assouline's version of a 'Cabinet de Curiosité', where you can purchase Assouline's art, chairs, lamps, carpets, sofas and desks. They'll even design an entire library for you, should you desire—cabinets and all. If you can't afford the library, or even the books, there are 'Library Candles' that smell of paper, leather or wood to recreate the atmosphere of a book-lined hideaway. And if it's all too much, retreat to the bar downstairs to rest your senses, where you can sip a G&T, champagne or a calming tea while browsing a book, or three.

196A Piccadilly, London. www.assouline.com

Clockwise from top left Heywood Hill catalogue; *Assouline's new London flagship store, Maison Assouline, on Piccadilly; Heywod Hill parcels for the late Duchess of Devonshire*

BOOKS FOR COOKS This place is not only a bookshop that feels good to walk into, with its bookshelves groaning with luscious cookbooks, it also smells fantastic! This is because there's a kitchen in the store and almost every day the space exudes appetising aromas that swirl enticingly around the tables and book piles. The small open space is terrific for a bite to eat, serving lunch from Tuesday to Saturday, and if you're not hungry upon entering, you soon will be! (There are also cooking classes, if you're keen to try the book receipes yourself, without waiting until you get home.) But this place is more than just a café with bookshelves: it also has a fantastic history. Those who have worked in the store include renowned food writer and cookbook author Annie Bell, and TV star Clarissa Dickson Wright. Writer Sophie Grigson also has an attachment after filming in the store. In fact, so many chefs and food writers gravitate here that you're likely to see a few when you wander in. (You'll be able to tell them by the piles of books they're collecting as they're walking around the shelves.) It's convivial, charming and still going strong, after all these years. A lovely tasty, little place. (Note that it's only open Tuesday to Saturday.)

4 Blenheim Crescent, Notting Hill, London. www.booksforcooks.com

This page from left to right *Books for Cooks*
Opposite *Henry Sotheran in Mayfair*
Following pages *Daunt Books in Marylebone*

CLAIRE DE ROUEN Charing Cross Road was once famous for its bookstores. (Remember the classic book *84 Charing Cross Road*?) In the 1990s, there was still a decent number of these lovely old bookstores left but now, in 2016, that number has, rather sadly, dwindled dramatically to only a few. Nevertheless, there are still some literary corners to lose yourself in, and one of them is Claire de Rouen. Tucked above William Hill, Claire de Rouen is one of the few specialist photography, art and fashion bookshops in London. (Potterton Books is another.) There are hundreds of titles here, from photography to fashion, design, limited-edition books and rare and signed titles, as well as international magazines and artist publications. The owner has a discerning eye and chooses books that are a little different from the mainstream, making it a great place to shop for fashion and design friends. The store is so highly regarded that book signings, magazine launches and artist projects are held here: past events have included Tim Walker, Juergen Teller, Bill Henson and Studio Voltaire. The store's innovative director, Lucy Kumara Moore, even started a new book fair in 2014, called Room&Book, which takes place in late May or early June every year.

125 Charing Cross Road, Soho, London.

DAUNT BOOKS Daunt is a very handsome bookstore, as famous for its Edwardian architecture and its British-racing-green branding as it is for its enormous, glass-ceiling and its extensive collection of travel titles. For years, this was where people came to buy guides on far-flung destinations, perhaps Mauritius, or Papua New Guinea, or Angkor Wat. Wherever you were heading, Daunt had the book to suit. Then, when the internet began offering travel info for free, Daunt diversified into other genres, although it continued to specialise in travel books. Today, it's still a beacon of hope for people trying to find details about destinations, whether it's walking holidays of the French Riviera or drinking holidays in Vegas. Books are arranged by city and country, rather than alphabetically, so guides, maps, non-fiction and fiction all sit alongside one another. It's a brilliant idea: when you want insights into Paris, there are all sorts of enticing guides, from expat memoirs to shopping titles. All of these tempting travel books sit at the back of the store, under an astonishingly beautiful glass roof and surrounded by a carved timber mezzanine. The rest of the store is for other genres, from fashion to design to philosophy. A great place to browse, even if you're not going anywhere.

83–84 Marylebone High Street, Marylebone, London.

124 **GOLDSBORO BOOKS** If you haven't wandered down Cecil Court, here's your opportunity. This bookstore dubs itself as "the UK's leading specialist in signed first editions" and it's a great place to source a really special gift to give a bookish friend—or yourself. First editions are one thing, but signed first editions another altogether, and the prices can reflect the difference. Then again, these kinds of books are collector's items, and usually increase in value over the years.

23–25 Cecil Court, London. www.goldsborobooks.com

HATCHARD'S Britain's oldest bookshop, Hatchard's is handily situated adjacent to the Wolseley brasserie on Piccadilly, so you can walk out of one and straight into the other. (Nothing like having a drink with your new book purchases!) The bookstore is becoming renowned for its excellent online catalogue, but many fans still like to come here in person, to browse the shelves and smell the scent of paper and possibility. If you're a collector, ask for the recently signed books. There are always lots of signed editions in store, which make for great gifts. Current stock includes Stephen Fry, Nigella Lawson, Ian McEwan, Ruth Rendell, Michel Roux, and Colm Toibin. Oh, and it has a Royal Warrant too, so obviously Buckingham Palace up the road is on the mailing list too!

187 Piccadilly, London. www.hatchards.co.uk

HENRY SOTHERAN Staffed by kindly gentleman (young and old), this grand old bookstore has been trading in London since 1761. It's the kind of London bookstore you long to find: an enormous room lined with beautiful old timber bookshelves and tables piled high with all kinds of lovely books, from curious old vintage gardening titles to long-forgotten biographies that are still interesting and of course great classics. Subjects cover natural history, architecture and travel. And if you love old prints, wander downstairs, where decorative prints in pristine condition are kept in map chests or display cabinets. I loved the 1930s travel posters for the French Riviera. The botanical prints make great gifts for gardeners.

2–5 Sackville Street, Mayfair, London. www.sotherans.uk

HEYWOOD HILL Ah, Heywood Hill. Mention these words to any book lover and it's likely their eyes will glaze with adoration. It's a tiny bookshop barely bigger than a pocket handkerchief—manager Nicky Dunne calls it the "biggest little bookshop in the world"—but it's packed with history, and not just that contained within its books' pages. This is where Nancy Mitford worked for a period during World War II, after owner Heywood Hill had signed up and before Nancy realised being in business wasn't

as fun as writing books. (Nancy had a financial stake in the store; her sister, Deborah Devonshire and her husband, the Duke of Devonshire, later bought it to keep it from going under.) It's where the Queen buys most of her reading. Hugh Grant too—although he does it under a nom de plume. Staff are wonderful in that dithery, bookshop-y way; bustling about trying to find obscure titles on goodness-knows-what for some lord-someone-or-another who's just popped in on his lunchbreak. The store is endearingly loyal to its customers: I reserved two signed editions of Cecil Beaton books, flew back to Australia and forgot about them until a year later. When I rang to enquire, they were still there, tucked away on the top shelf. The store stocks all the newest titles but there are quite a few antiquarian books, too. Heywood's staff say they endeavour to find "interesting books"; especially if they're beautiful or quirky. The store's strength is English literature and English history, but there are great art, architecture, travel and gardening titles, too. Each purchase is exquisitely wrapped in Heywood's elegant white tissue paper and finished with a navy-blue ribbon. (A third of the store's customers live in the US and no doubt appreciate the quintessentially British navy branding as much as the Heywood Hill heritage.) It's all very elegant, very gracious, and very pleasurable. They'll even curate your private library, if you don't have the time to do it yourself.

10 Curzon St, Mayfair, London. www.heywoodhill.com

IDEA BOOKS This small, independent seller of books and magazines is one of those places that tends to sit under the retail radar. It's known to bookish insiders—architects, designers and the like—but only slowly coming to the attention of 'outsiders,' too. It began as a boutique operation that quietly supplied the design world with rare and out-of-print editions, largely through a small office in Soho, but such was its success that it's now expanded to a corner of the Dover Street Market deprtment stores, with an outpost in New York. People such as Bruce Weber and the editors of Condé Nast frequent IDEA for ideas (naturally), while others rely on the founders for suggesting great gifts or unusual design, art and photography books.

101 Wardour Street, Soho, London. www.ideanow.online

Opposite *John Sandoe Books in Chelsea*

JOHN SANDOE BOOKS One of the best-loved and longest-surviving independent bookshops in London, John Sandoe's celebrated shop is in the same league as Heywood Hill; it's almost an icon of the city, certainly for book lovers. This distinguished bookstore (the jet-black façade gives the first indication that it's a rather impressive sort of space) has been here, just off King's Road in Chelsea, since 1957, when Chelsea still had greengrocers and corner stores, rather than high street chains. Before it was a bookstore it was a poodle parlour, and John Sandoe's upper-class stockbroker father thought he was crazy to open in such a place, on such a side street, in such a dubious neighbourhood. (Chelsea hadn't yet started swinging but it was still pretty boho and raffish in places.) John Sandoe's dream was to tailor books to its customers, rather than offer any old jacketed rubbish, and it worked: buyers were so taken with the service and the customisation they kept returning year after year, decade after decade. (Sundays began at 6am, when staff would head out to deliver orders in time for their customers' breakfasts.) Regulars included fashion designer Mary Quant, Keith Richards, Lucian Freud, Dirk Bogarde and Tom Stoppard. Katharine Hepburn was shooed away from the window because they thought she was a drunk hobo. In 1989 John Sandoe sold the shop (which retained his name) to three colleagues and customers and retired to Dorset. He died in 2008. However, his legacy and his service still live on at this very fine bookstore, which has become something of a mecca for book lovers from all four corners of the world. Some people simply step inside to pay their respects, take a wistful look, and then continue on their merry way.

10 Blacklands Terrace, Chelsea, London. www.johnsandoe.com

LUYTENS & RUBINSTEIN Wonderful name, wonderful store! This is an elegant bookshop, marked by a sophisticated black-and-white striped exterior awning in summer, and a cosy-looking, beautifully lit interior in winter. Even the sign is beautiful. It's a relatively new independent store, founded in 2009 by established literary agents. Because its owners are au fait with the game, there are all sorts of intelligent titles here, with an emphasis on highbrow non-fiction. However, there's also a broad range of titles in art, poetry and children's books, as well as other genres. Look out for the sliding bookcases in the basement to add a touch drama to your browsing.

21 Kensington Park Road, Notting Hill, London. www.lutyensrubinstein.co.uk

PERSEPHONE BOOKS Persephone is that unusual combination of a bookshop and a publisher, but what makes it even more unusual is that it publishes, or rather reprints, neglected fiction and non-fiction from the early part of the 20th century. Now before you sigh and think ho hum, reserve judgement because Persephone's little titles brim over with personality and pleasure. Some of the 112 titles include: *The Making of a Marchioness*, an "unromantic romance" by author Frances Hodgson Burnett (who wrote *The Secret Garden*), which Nancy Mitford supposedly loved; *Kitchen Essays* by Agnes Jekyll, (sister-in-law to Gertrude); *Cheerful Weather for the Wedding* by Bloomsbury Set author Julia Strachey (niece of Lytton), which became a beautiful film; *The Wise Virgins*, a semi-autobiographical tale by Leonard Woolf about his wife Virginia, and the wittily titled *Gardener's Nightcap* by Muriel Stuart. These are books that are neither too literary nor too commercial, but 'just right'; stories that engage and entertain in myriad ways. But perhaps the loveliest thing of all about these books is that each is covered in an elegant grey jacket and features a 'fabric' endpaper with matching bookmark. Truly delightful.

59 Lamb's Conduit Street, Bloomsbury, London. www.persephonebooks.co.uk

Above *Potterton Books*
Opposite clockwise from top left *Lutyens & Rubinstein;*
John Sandoe Books; Heywood Hill; Persephone Books

PETER HARRINGTON If bookstores have personalities, then Peter Harrington is the serious, bespectacled, nose-in-the-pages intellectual; the lover of highbrow and books that speak (and smell) of history, mystery and marvellous things. The strength of this bookstore is its antiquarian books. The store was established in 1969 and has become one of the leading rare-books firms in the world, selling from two stores in Mayfair and Fulham Road, Chelsea, as well as at international book and antiques fairs all around the world. While both of the London stores are enticing, it's the Fulham Road one that perhaps has more atmosphere (by a smidgeon). Grand timber bookshelves, long leaning ladders and tweed-coated, felt-hat-wearing gentlemen poring over first editions make you realise this is a serious bookstore indeed. The shelves include rare and valuable books from the 15th to 20th centuries, including a publisher's copy of Mark Twain's *Huckleberry Finn* (supposedly the first copy ever bound), Virginia Woolf's pocket engagement diaries, and a signed first edition of a Vita Sackville West garden book, which was displayed in a window of horticultural titles during Chelsea Flower Show week. The illustrated catalogues are like sumptuous magazines in themselves. Peter Harrington passed away in 2003, but his son Pom (great name!) still runs the family business in the same way, with old-fashioned service and magnificent books to read. A glorious place that reminds you how beautiful bookstores used to be.

100 Fulham Road, Chelsea, London; 43 Dover Street, Mayfair, London. www.peterharrington.co.uk

POTTERTON BOOKS One of the best bookstores in London, if not the world, for second-hand architecture, design and garden titles, Potterton is an endearing treasure tucked away behind Sloane Square. Conveniently, it's on the route to the Chelsea Flower Show so you can easily pop in before or after the show, and it always has beautiful garden-themed windows during Chelsea Week. It always has the latest and best design and garden books on its front table, and the selection is always interesting—a pleasing combination of small and independent publishers and the big-brand names. But Potterton's real strength is its second-hand books; it really does have the best selection of old and vintage interior design and garden titles, most of which are in beautiful condition. Ask to peek at the back shelf for the extremely rare and extremely old garden books. And don't miss the display shelves where the enormous garden and design tomes sit like elegant still lifes. There are always lovely finds here—last time there was a little pile of Laura Stoddart's gorgeous illustrated garden books, all signed by her on a recent visit. Big windows, eye-catching merchandising, kind staff; the best kind of bookshop, really.

93 Lower Sloane Street, Chelsea, London. www.pottertonbookslondon.com

SHAPERO RARE BOOKS Shapero Rare Books is one of London's leading antiquarian bookshops. It specialises in travel, natural history, English literature and continental books. But what most collectors come here for are the rare editions. These, along with the antique maps and vintage photographs, are just enthralling. Try to resist! The store also does valuations if you have books to sell.

32 St George Street, London. shapero.com

SOUTH KENSINGTON BOOKS A quiet gem near the South Kensington tube, this sweet spot is great for a browse if you have a few moments before heading to the V&A or catching a train for home. It's well-laid-out but narrow in width, making navigating the tables an obstacle course. But oh, what a lovely one! Every table groans with titles. And the store always seems to be FULL—with both locals and commuters browsing for their next train read. It's best for interesting new bibliographies, political books, satire and quirky titles, but there are also good art, architecture and design titles, many of which sit on the main table in the front of the store—a sign of the book's proximity to the V&A.

22 Thurloe Street, South Kensington, London. www.kensingtonbooks.co.uk

THE SOCIETY CLUB Billing itself as "the best of all possible things", the Society Club at is really a bookshop that hides a members' club, that, in turn, hides all manner of lovely things. It's also an art space and a modern salon. In short, a place for creative people to get together, read books, chat and have a drink. Run by literary agent Carrie Kania and interior designer Babette Kulik, it began as an independent bookstore / art gallery specialising in 20th-century literature, art and visual culture from modernism to the contemporary, but then quickly morphed into a kind of 'club'-meets-bookstore / general store selling lots of lovely things from vintage first-edition books to great old furniture to limited-edition prints, and even homemade jam and other delicious stuff. A communal table runs through the centre of the shop, aiming to bring like-minded people together and encourage the 'intellectual cool' to mingle over tea, coffee, pastries and cakes. There are always book launches, poetry readings, storytelling and live music sessions. One great event was a Q&A with Andy Warhol's friend and the Factory's in-house photographer, Leee Black Childers. There's also a sister version in Shoreditch at 3 Cheshire Street.

12 Ingestre Place, Soho, London.

Opposite *The Society Club*

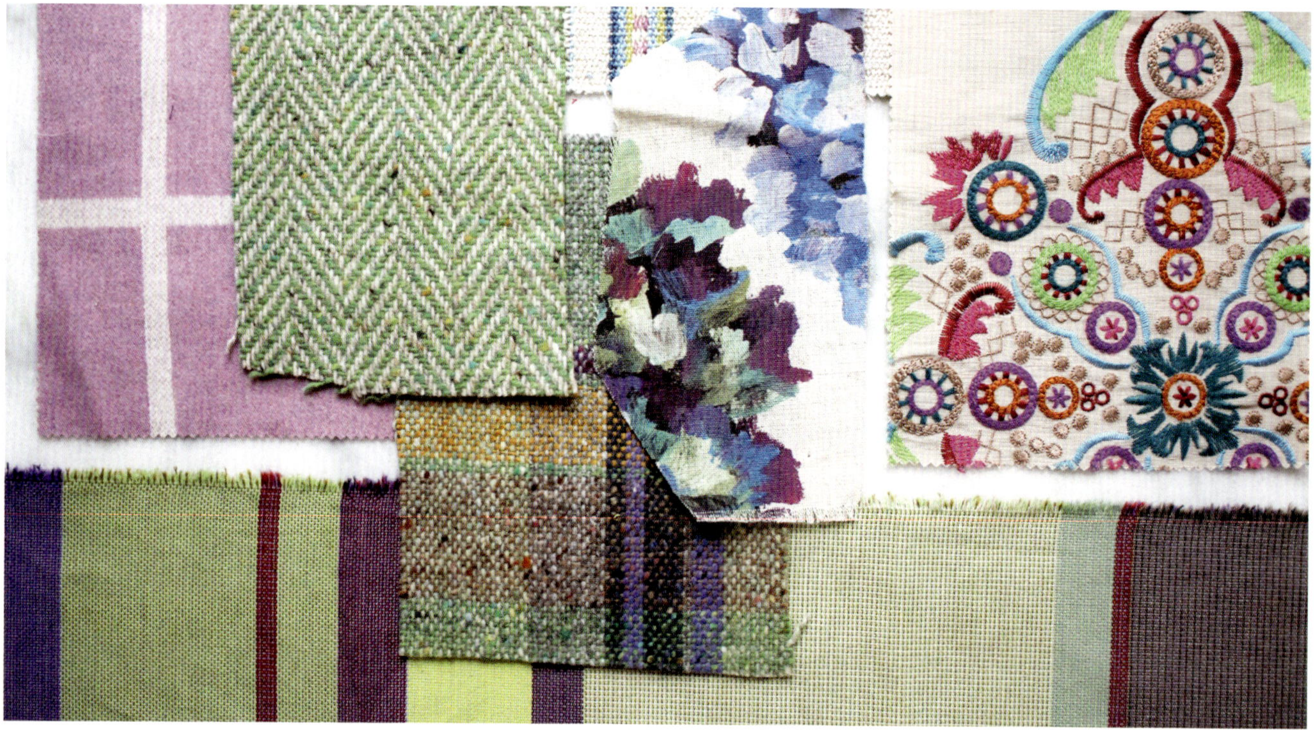

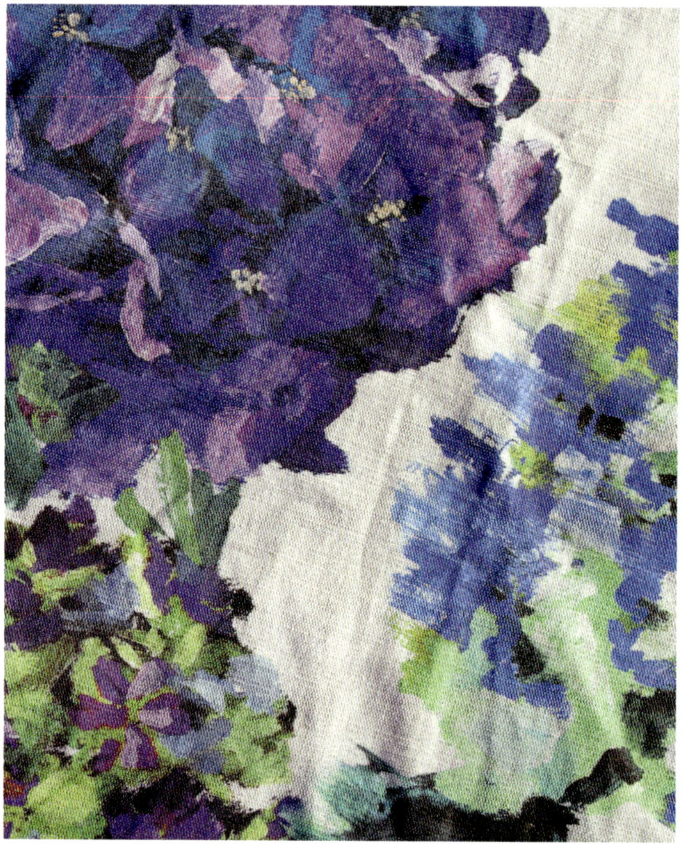

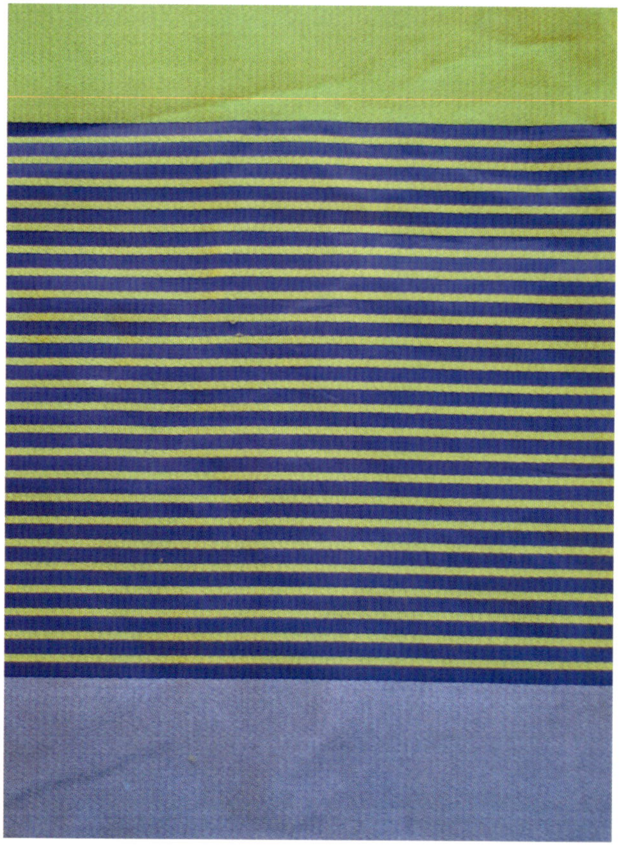

FABRICS AND TEXTILES

BERWICK STREET Although this is an entire street and not just one store, I'm including it because it's full of fabric sellers. They're dotted all down the street and in the side lanes too, so meander down and get lost among all the lovely traders. The two stores of the famous Cloth House are here (see entry in this section), as well as Silk Society, Misan Textiles (two stores), Biddle Sawyer Silks, and Borovick. Kleins on Noel Street (just around the corner) also has an amazing selection of trimmings to match your fabric purchases. Prices can be high and the friendliness of staff varies, but they're all worth a browse as you never know what you'll find. Some of the guipure laces are exquisite.

Berwick Street, Soho, London.

CABBAGES AND ROSES The cutely named Cabbages and Roses has an army of fans as long as King's Road. It used to operate out of a very pretty shopfront down the Fulham end of King's Road but has now moved to an even prettier premise on Sydney Street, conveniently closer to all the action. It's a fashion boutique but half its business is fabrics and textiles. Founder Christina Strutt is fond of florals and this is the place to come if you love linens with huge swirls of flowers growing from one end to the other. There are two prints, the Hatley Rose and the Catherine Rose, both gorgeous, romantic and utterly covetable. There are also ticking stripes and other patterns, but it's the flowers people fall for. Elsewhere in the store are equally irresistible homewares: cushions, candles, ornaments and of course the famous Cabbages and Roses frocks—part Edwardian, part summer garden party.

121–123, Sydney Street, Chelsea, London. www.cabbagesandroses.com

Opposite clockwise from top *Fabric samples at Chelsea Harbour; navy stripes from Designers Guild; hydrangeas design from Designers Guild*
Following pages from left to right *Cushions from Designers Guild; trims for Samuel and Sons at Chelsea Harbour Design Centre*

CHELSEA HARBOUR DESIGN CENTRE The vast Chelsea Harbour Design Centre comprises three large glass-domed areas filled with light and space, which are supplemented by an additional set of showrooms across a walkway. Because of its design, it's a serene, immediately calming environment, perfectly suited to hours spent peering in windows and poring over fabrics. There are more than 100 showrooms here trading in fabrics, trims and other passementerie. Some of my favourites are Tissus d'Hélène (a wonderful, stylish jumble of beautiful tactile fabrics), Brunschwig & Fils, Kravet, GP and J Baker, and Samuel and Sons. Some are trade-only, but you can ask for samples of your preferred fabrics to take back to your interior designer to order. And if you need a break from browsing fabrics, there's a lovely café, which has an accompanying bookshop full of specialist design, fashion and garden titles.

Design Centre, Chelsea Harbour, Lots Road, Chelsea, London.
www.dcch.co.uk

CHELSEA TEXTILES Chelsea Textiles has been covered a lot in the international media in recent years because of its involvement with Kit Kemp and her interiors in the Firmdale Hotels, but the company was also doing wonderful things before Ms Kemp highlighted its talents. The company was formed by Mona Perlhagen in 1992 to recreate and thus preserve the beauty and art of antique textiles, particularly embroidered textiles, the originals of which were becoming scarce. Mona Perlhagen has previously been a fashion buyer for Bloomingdale's in New York, but moved to London where the market for perfect recreations of antique embroidered fabrics to complement traditional interiors was bigger, and perhaps more appreciative. She set about sourcing authentic hand-embroidered fabrics from the 17th and 18th centuries, and then found the world's best craftsmen to reproduce them. The company now sells these designs alongside Gustavian furniture (which seems to suit them perfectly). Staff also offer an interior design and bespoke service, which Kit Kemp has famously used. Every year, there's an annual sale in mid-November at the Chelsea Town Hall, which sells both one-of-a-kind samples as well as the company's main range.

13 Walton Street, Chelsea, London. www.chelseatextiles.com/uk

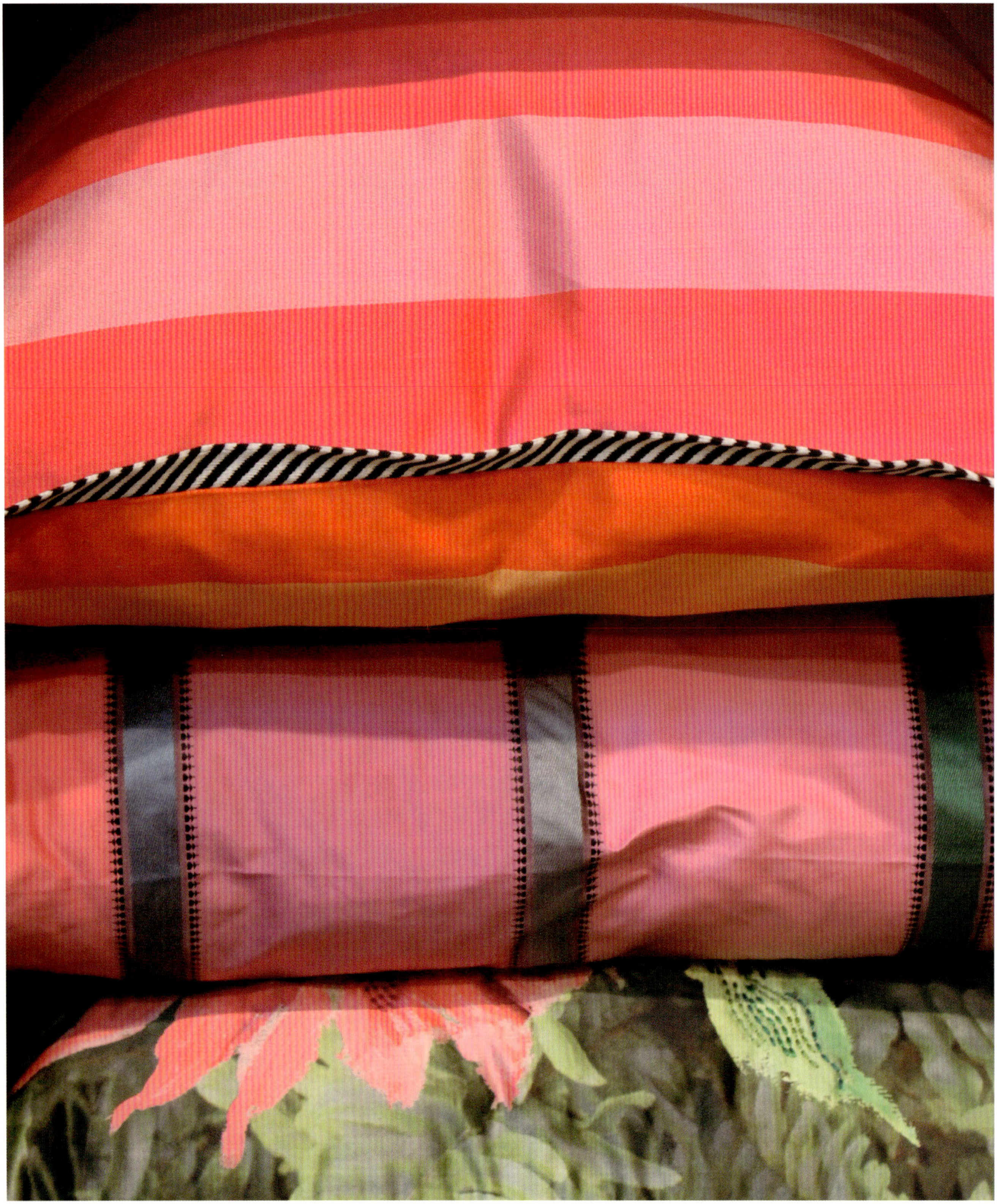

134

COLEFAX AND FOWLER Colefax and Fowler, is, along with Designers Guild, one of my first stops whenever I arrive in London. While Designers Guild is more about colour and texture, Colefax and Fowler is more about quiet French glamour and understated English elegance. There's a great range of fabrics in this showroom, but perhaps the most beautiful designs are those from French textile house Manuel Canovas. Whether embroidered, printed or quietly sophisticated, Manuel Canovas' range is just sublime. (And better still, you don't need a designer's trade card to shop here, although you do need to allow a few days for your order to process, as the stock is housed elsewhere.) If you can't afford the fabrics at full price, bear in mind that once a year, in January, Colefax and Fowler have a huge sale to clear all their stock, which includes not only their own label but also high-end fabrics from Jane Churchill, Manuel Canovas and Larsen. It's held in the Royal Horticultural Society (RHS) hall in Victoria, with up to 70 per cent off normal prices. Plus, you can find discontinued lines and smaller remnants from the current ranges, including prints (cotton, linen union), silks, sheers, velvets, damask and other good finds. All Colefax and Fowler, Manuel Canovas and Larsen fabrics are prices at a fixed £26 per metre, Jane Churchill fabrics are £20 per metre. People go a little crazy at this sale. It's easy to see why. It's a fabric-lover's fantasy.
110 Fulham Road, Chelsea, London. www.colefax.com

DESIGNERS GUILD Confession: Designers Guild is a bit of a mecca for me. It's often the first place I go to when I arrive in London. And I always—always—buy something. (Tip: It's a good idea to go here early in your London stay because the fabrics can often take a few days to be delivered from the warehouse; but staff will call when they're ready to be collected.) This is the celebrated company created by Tricia Guild in 1970 that's still going strong today, mostly because of its glorious, gorgeous, eye-poppingly colourful fabrics. Honestly, you can't imagine a place that's more like a candy store for haberdashery fans. Flicking through the dozens of catalogues and collections is even better than going through a seed catalogue if you're a gardener. There's everything from the unbelievably romantic rose prints and flocked velvet to the sleek understated linens here, although the more popular designs are, not surprisingly, the ornate patterns. Many of the fabrics are hung in a system of giant hangers placed around the showroom, so you can fully see the prints and feel the textures, but as there are so many collections, others can only be seen as swatches, or as photos in the catalogues. The King's

Road store and the one in Marylebone are the only places in the world where the public can walk in and buy without a trade card, so it can get a little busy. But that's OK, because you'll be too preoccupied with trying to decide on your favourites anyway! Don't miss the cushions at the back of the store, the offcut bin of bargain bits, and the whole bolts, where you can buy lengths of fabric then and there, without having to wait several days for delivery. There are two stores on King's Road in Chelsea; one is dedicated to fabrics and the other is for homewares, with some fabrics downstairs. As well as the Designers Guild collections, the stores carry the likes of Ralph Lauren Home and Jasper Conran—some designs of which are exclusive to the store.
267–277 King's Road, Chelsea, London. www.designersguild.com

IAN MANKIN You know those sofas you see in magazines and books that have been slip-covered in bold gingham-style checks? The kind we all thought went out in the 1980s but are now clearly back in, as evidenced by Furlow Gatewood's bestselling book? Well, one man in London is the king of check. Ian Mankin has been selling simple, striped check and stripe fabrics for decades now. The difference between his and the old cheapie check is that he reinterprets these classic patterns by putting them onto linens and heavy-duty upholstery and curtain fabrics. He does lots of other fabrics, but checks are his main seller. And why not? They look fantastic. The pale blues are particularly beautiful.
271–273 Wandsworth Bridge Road, Fulham, London. www.ianmankin.co.uk

Opposite clockwise from top left *The Designers Guild showroom on King's Road; a fabric from Robert Allen at the Chelsea Harbour Design Centre; The Cloth Shop in Notting Hill; a Manuel Canovas design at Colefax and Fowler*

JOEL AND SONS This store is on Church Street, off Edgware Road, so you have to do a little trek to find it. But it's worth the walk. It's a family-owned business that began right opposite its current location, in a humble fabric stall, and has grown to become an internationally known source of splendid textiles and trims. The family has connections with factories in Italy, France, Switzerland and India, so there are always interesting fabrics here. It also sells a staggering selection of other sewing materials, including patterns by designer brands, plus all of the trimmings. Look out for the bins full of amazing offcuts. If you go on Saturday, there is also a fabric stall in the market on Church Street that sells silks and Liberty cotton at a third of the usual price—one of the best market stalls selling fabrics in London. Nearby, there is also Jason Fabrics and Hadson Fabrics, both on Edgware Road.

73–87 Church Street, Lisson Grove, London. www.joelandsonfabrics.com

LIBERTY Let's be honest; Liberty doesn't have the fabric department it used to boast, before it had that big makeover and chucked out all the old-fashioned departments and their seemingly out-of-date stock. And there are many of us who miss it. We used to go into Liberty just to walk around the bolts. However, it *has* retained its famous cotton prints, including the floral, peacock and paisley patterns. There are also contemporary fabric designers such as Osborne & Little and smaller brands such as Hibou Home. Still worth a browse, if only to experience that glorious building.

Regent Street, West End, London. www.liberty.co.uk

MACCULLOCH AND WALLIS A serious haberdasher for serious seamstresses (and tailors), this impressive multistorey store off Oxford Street is intimidating at first, with gorgeous window displays, grand antique counters and expensive-looking fabrics, but don't let the look of it unnerve you. The staff are wonderful (I've never had a bad experience here!), and the fabrics even better. Everything is of the highest quality, from the feathers to the lace. It's famous for finding and stocking some of the most unusual fabrics and therefore is frequented by local London College of Fashion students. The fabric rolls include Nicole Fabre's exquisite hand-printed linens inspired by French antique textiles, but there's also 292-centimetre-wide (115-inch-wide) white Irish linen sheeting (very rare), so you can sew your own hotel-style bed linen.

25–26 Dering Street (off Oxford Street), London. www.macculloch-wallis.co.uk

PONGEES Such a quirky name! But then, being in Spitalfields, where quirky is the name of the game, it makes sense. It's also a perfect place for a silk store, with London's Spitalfields having been the home of Huguenot silk weaver refugees, who settled in the 17th century. Now its main stock is silk, so don't go expecting a range of fabrics. But there are also other elegant evening fabrics, such as crepe georgette, French chiffon, velvet, taffeta, tulle and crepe satin. (The crepe georgettes are glorious; always a superb fabric for flowing party frocks.) These are high-end, high-fashion dress silks, coveted for the colours and texture. Designed in-house, the pigment-dye and embroidered ranges are produced in India, and the colours will make you sigh with longing. Some of the most beautiful fabrics are the embroidery collection; they look like something Dries van Noten would use, or Raf Simons when he was at Dior.

28/30 Hoxton Square, Spitalfields, London. www.pongees.co.uk

REDLOH HOUSE FABRICS To locate this cute place, look for the cute mews just off the New King's Road and then the even cuter blue-shuttered cottage. Owned and run by Nicole Pritchard-Smith, it's a relaxed space that implores you to feel the fabrics. The fabric designers stocked include Astrid & Rudolf, Penny Morrison, Carolina Irving and Christine Van Der Hurd, whose career began in the 1970s designing for Yves Saint Laurent.

2 Michael Road, Chelsea, London. www.redlohhousefabrics.com

RUSSELL & CHAPPLE Known as the secret source for extra-wide (up to 300 centimetres or 118 inches) plain cotton and linen fabrics suitable for curtains and upholstery, R&C has great selections that include herringbone, 100 per cent Belgian linen, pretty ivory linens woven in Scotland, 'half Panama' pre-washed cottons, and 'butter' muslins. And for curtains in danger from egg-wielding theatre critics, R&C also stocks stain-resistant Teflon-coated linens.

68 Drury Lane, Soho, London. www.russellandchapple.co.uk

THE CLOTH HOUSE What haber fan doesn't know about this heavenly place? There are two Cloth Houses, but the one at the northern end of Berwick Street (closer to Oxford Street) is perhaps the best, or at least the one with the most atmosphere. Old timber shelves groaning with lovely bolts of linen; walls papered in vintage *Vogue* patterns, bins full of fantastic French bits and bobs … it's like a wonderful old general store, but one designed for sewers and crafters. Always good stuff here. Don't miss the heavy-duty French and Belgium linens at the back; the colours are superb!

47 and 98 Berwick Street, Soho, London. www.clothhouse.com

THE CLOTH SHOP Portobello Road isn't known for textile and fabric stores—they're really more associated with King's Road, Fulham Road and Soho, but this cute buttonhole of a place seems to fit in with Notting Hill's aesthetic. It's full to the brim with beautiful bolts, ribbons, threads and passementerie galore. It's slightly difficult to walk through all the stock, which makes it all the more enthralling. The best fabrics are the Swedish linens—152-centimetre-wide (60-inch-wide), medium-weight, real (imported) Swedish linen in 45 colours, but there are also heavyweight Indian furnishing cottons and other fabrics, plus pretty ribbons and trims. The wool blankets are pretty covetable as well. On weekends, there is a stall outside, with more haberdashery treasures, including some vintage stock.

290 Portobello Road, Notting Hill, London. www.theclothshop.net

TISSUS D'HÉLÈNE Tissus d'Hélène is a cute name (*tissus* means fabric in French) for an even more delightful showroom. Everything looks so lovely here, from the delightful Swedish- and French-style cabinets piled high with carefully folded lengths of hand-blocked and hand-screen-printed fabrics to the friendly girls serving customers. It's one of the most appealing places to shop for fabric in London. Hand-screen-printed fabrics are the main textiles here, but there is also a huge range of other kinds of fabrics from dozens of leading designers. It's a must-see stop for those seeking beautiful fabrics that are a little different from all the patterns being bandied about in design land.

Fourth Floor Design Centre East, Chelsea Harbour Design Centre, Lots Road, Chelsea, London. www.tissusdhelene.co.uk

TURNELL & GIGNON If you're a fabric fan and you haven't yet stepped inside the Design Centre at Chelsea Harbour, then get yourself there quick smart! You won't want to go anywhere else after you've seen this extravaganza of silk and tweed and linen and trims. There are more than 100 stores here and the quirkily named Turnell & Gignon is one of the best. It stocks some of the finest fabrics from high-end fabric houses and celebrated international designers, including Mary McDonald's Chinoiserie collection for Schumacher; Nicky Haslam's cotton velvet collection; Neisha Crosland's Weave Collection; and Edmund Petit, which is now responsible for Madeleine Castaing's fabric designs. Lots here to keep you happy for an hour or more.

Chelsea Harbour Design Centre, Lots Road, Chelsea, London.
www.turnellandgigongroup.com

From opposite left to right *French grosgrain ribbons at VV Rouleaux; Spring linens at Designers Guild; trims at Chelsea Harbour Design Centre's window displays; bolts at the Cloth House*

VV ROULEAUX This is an enchanting store dedicated to trims and ribbons and other pretty things for sewing. There are feathers and faux flowers galore (great for racing hats or embellishing dresses), but there are also beads, tassels and every kind of ribbon imaginable. Don't miss the downstairs area, where there are often bargain bins full of fabrics.
102 Marylebone Lane (off Marylebone High Street), Marylebone London. www.vvrouleaux.com

WILLIAM YEOWARD I'm tempted to do what esteemed guidebook reviewers used to do in their books when they didn't want the world knowing about a great find and hide this all the way down the list, but it already is, due to the 'W' in the name! William Yeoward's store is just sublime—almost as divine as the staff inside it. There are luscious cushions and homewares galore, but they pale beside the fabrics, which are some of the most beautiful in London. From ornate velvets to embroidered linens, you'll find whatever you need here to make your home look like a magazine spread.
270 King's Road, Chelsea, London. www.williamyeoward.com

Opposite clockwise from top left *The Cloth House in Soho; MacCulloch & Wallis; VV Rouleaux; The Cloth House*
Above *The window at the Cloth House*
Left *Cabbages and Roses in Chelsea*

This page *William Yeoward homewares*
Opposite *Ian Makin fabrics*

CREATIVE SPACES AND

DESTINATIONS

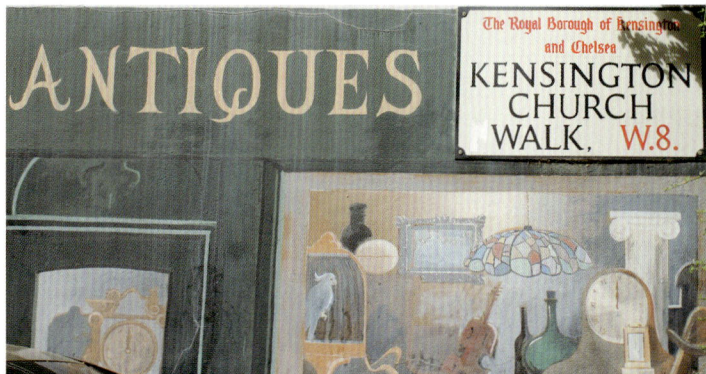

ANTIQUES

The Royal Borough of Kensington and Chelsea
KENSINGTON CHURCH WALK, W.8.

ENTREATH & HALL
ANTIQUES

TEL: 020 7584
WWW.BENTLEYSLONDON

ANTIQUES AND VINTAGE

ALFIE'S ANTIQUE MARKET Alfie's has been there for decades. And in that time, it's attracted a legion of fans, including Tom Dixon, Nina Campbell, Jasper Conran and Kelly Hoppen. It's well known among the trade and a few fashion celebrities, but, strangely, seems to have gone largely unnoticed by all but the savviest of Londoners and those foreigners in the design industry. And this is a problem, because the lack of attention is affecting business. Like many antiques and second-hand markets, Alfie's has changed dramatically over the years, as the market conditions and demand (or drop in demand) for antiques has changed. But it doesn't help when this location is a little off the beaten track. Many of the stall holders have moved into shops on Church Street or even gone to King's Road, where there are more upscale clients to sell to. However, there are still some 70 great stalls to look for beautiful things. And the quality is still high. New York designers such as Madeline Weinrib shop here for unusual pieces to take back to the US. That alone is a tick of approval for this place. Some of the best dealers to look for are the Italian dealers, Francesca Martire (www.francescamartire.com) and Vincenzo Caffarella (www.vinca.co.uk), on the ground floor. There are also always lovely things at Lorna Lee Leslie and Paolo Bonino. Louise Verber's stall on the second floor sells gorgeous glassware and mirrors, including wonderful large mirrored coasters that are meant to support vases. Outside, on Church Street, there are more dealers, including Andrew Nebbett (www.andrewnebbett.com), a great source for beautiful creamware and long oak dining tables. Some of the things to look out for at Alfie's are antique jewellery, antique tulipieres and other blue and white china, elegant silverware (of the kind you see in Ralph Lauren's Home stores), and 20th-century design, particularly lighting, all of which are starting to go for high prices again. Even if you are only browsing, the dealers are lovely and happy to share their knowledge.

13–25 Church Street, Lisson Grove, London.

www.alfiesantiques.com

ANTIQUE AND VINTAGE FLEA MARKET Every Thursday there's a flea market in Old Spitalfields, which is formally called the Thursday Antique and Vintage Flea Market but is mostly known as 'the flea market in Old Spitalfields'. It specialises in antiques and vintage wares of every kind, from furniture to William Morris prints. Many designers like to go to look around for inspiration for their work, but get there early if you want a bargain. There are the usual bits—vintage kitchenware, Georgian chaise lounges and so on—but there can be gems too, such as silverware and Art Deco treasures. Wayne Lawrence's store is particularly good for Victorian screens and 1930s steamer trunks.

Horner Square, Spitalfields, London. www.oldspitalfieldsmarket.com

BOURBON HANBY ARCADE A wonderful arcade of antiques that's often missed by travellers is the Bourbon Hanby Arcade, off King's Road in Chelsea. A discreet, petite little place, it feels a little like a Tardis: enter the door and be enthralled by a maze of stalls offering all kinds of treasures, from authentic Louis Vuitton steamer trunks to Hermès handbags, Chanel jewellery and beautiful silver trays and candlesticks.

151 Sydney Street, Chelsea, London.

www.bourbonhanby.com

CAMDEN PASSAGE The pedestrian lane of Camden Passage is famous for its antiques and vintage stores. The main market and trading days are Wednesdays and Saturdays, but many shops open weekdays or by arrangement. Note: Camden Passage, Islington, should not be confused with Camden Market or Camden Lock, which is in the neighbouring borough of Camden.

29 Camden Passage, Shoreditch, London.

Opposite clockwise from top left Luke Irwin on Pimlico Road; Pentreath & Hall; cute signage in Kensington; Bentleys in South Kensington; Pentreath & Hall

Staffordshire
Caanon £23.
PM - 14205

GOLBORNE ROAD Located north of and therefore slightly apart from the mess that is Portobello Road on a weekend, Golborne Road is where many of the more high-end dealers have decamped to in order to get away from, well, the madness a few blocks south. This small but serious pocket of antique loveliness is for serious buyers, with everything from vintage French bits to high-end pieces crammed into a tiny, teeny thoroughfare. Some of the boutiques worth browsing are Bazar Antiques for its Frenchy-chic furniture (82 Golborne Road); Les Couilles du Chien for great lamps, gilt frames, Murano chandeliers, antique chairs and tables (65 Golborne Road), and Hutch Interiors for midcentury chairs, French garden tables, Danish chairs, cocktail chairs, all kinds of chairs! (61 Golborne Road, London). Just off Golborne Road, Portobello Bookshop (328 Portobello Road) is filled with rare and out-of-print titles. But there are too many gorgeous stores to mention here, so make your way to Golborne Road (it's a wee hike from Portobello Road but worth it), and just wander in and out of the antiques dealers at your leisure. There's nothing lovelier on a Saturday afternoon in London.

PIMLICO ROAD Pimlico is prime antiques hunting territory. This is where a lot of London's upscale traders have moved to, thus creating a sophisticated little cluster of antiquery. There's Christopher Howe for manor-worthy pieces plus beautiful leather hides ready for furniture and also bespoke pieces (93 Pimlico Road, www.howelondon.com), there's Rose Uniacke, who has the loveliest, most delicate chandeliers, and elegant antiques to match, (76 Pimlico Road, ww.roseuniacke.com), and there's Luke Irwin, who has a gorgeous collection of handmade rugs (20–22 Pimlico Road, www.lukeirwin.com). And there are many other furniture and homeware stores, too, including Zuber (amazing wallpaper), Linley (divine furniture), and Nicholas Haslam (gracious, gorgeous pieces, including blue and white vases).

PORTOBELLO ROAD If you must go to Portobello Road on a Saturday, rise early to avoid the hoards. Alternatively, consider going on a Friday, when many of the shops and arcades are open—although there are fewer street vendors to browse. Some of the better stores and stalls to look out for are Henry Gregory (82 Portobello Road) for quintessentially British antiques, such as leather cases, vintage sporting gear and beautiful old prints; Atlam (11 Portobello Road) for seriously lovely silverware; and Barham Antiques (83 Portobello Road) for exquisite antique boxes in silver, bronze, etched glass, polished timber, and all sorts of other styles. But there are so many stalls and shops here that you're liable to find something you like. Just wander along Portobello Road and don't forget to venture down the little pedestrian passages; that's often where the best gems are!

This page *Henry Gregory on Portobello Road*
Opposite *A vintage tea set at Golborne Road*
Following pages from left to right *Susan Osborne's shop, part of the Golborne Road neighbourhood of antiques traders; Christopher Howe on Pimlico Road, part of Pimlico's thriving antiques scene*

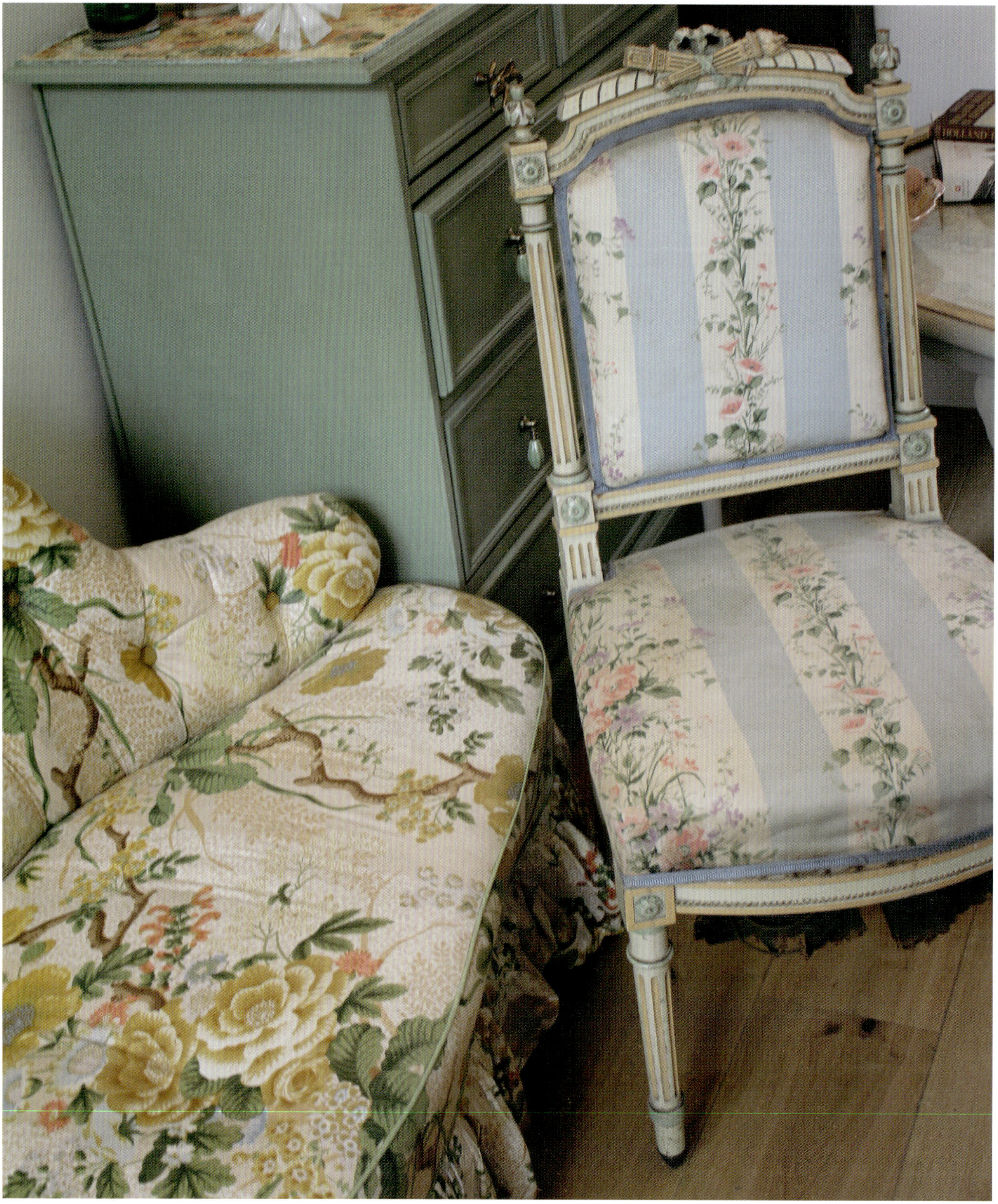

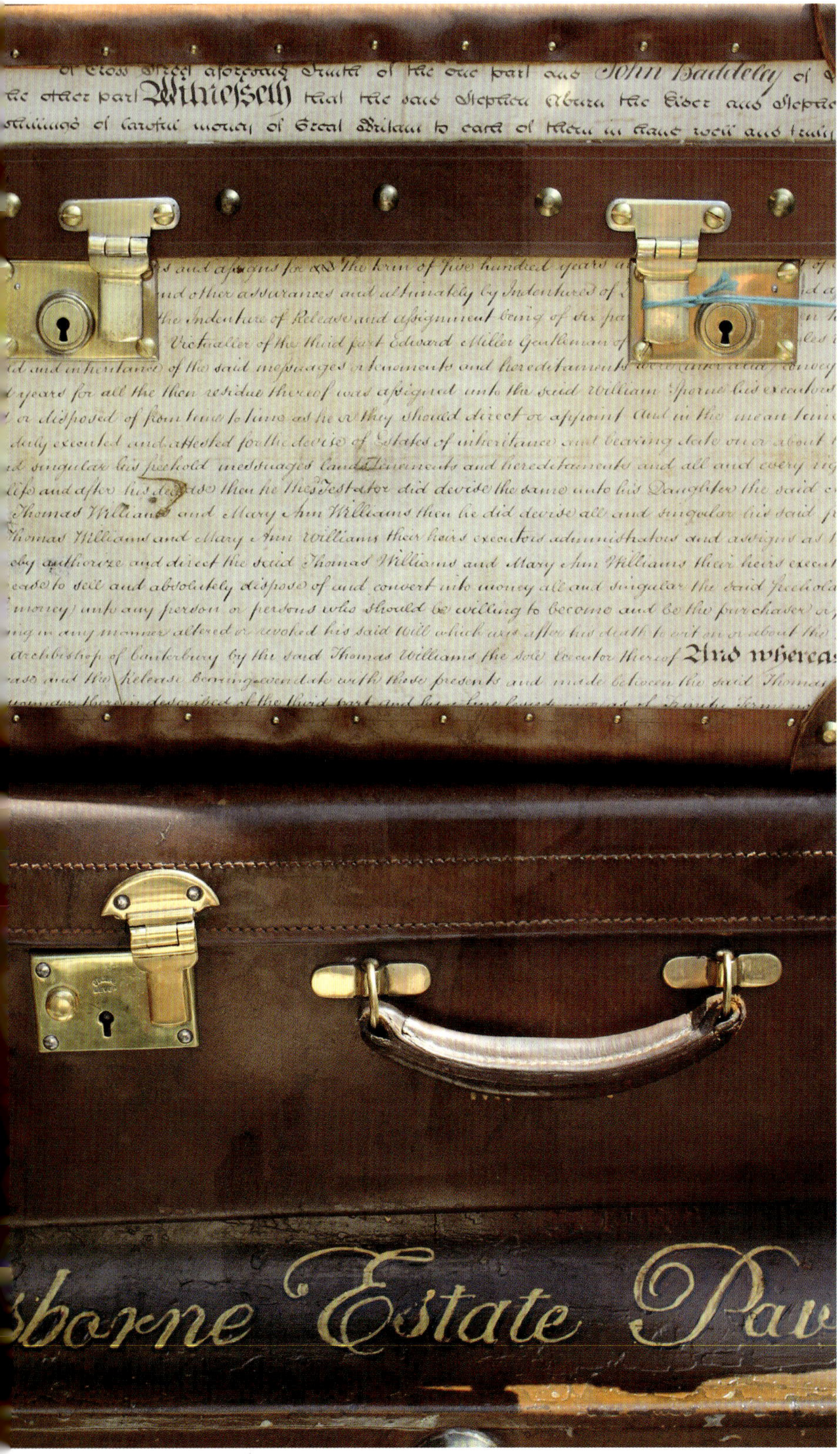
Estate

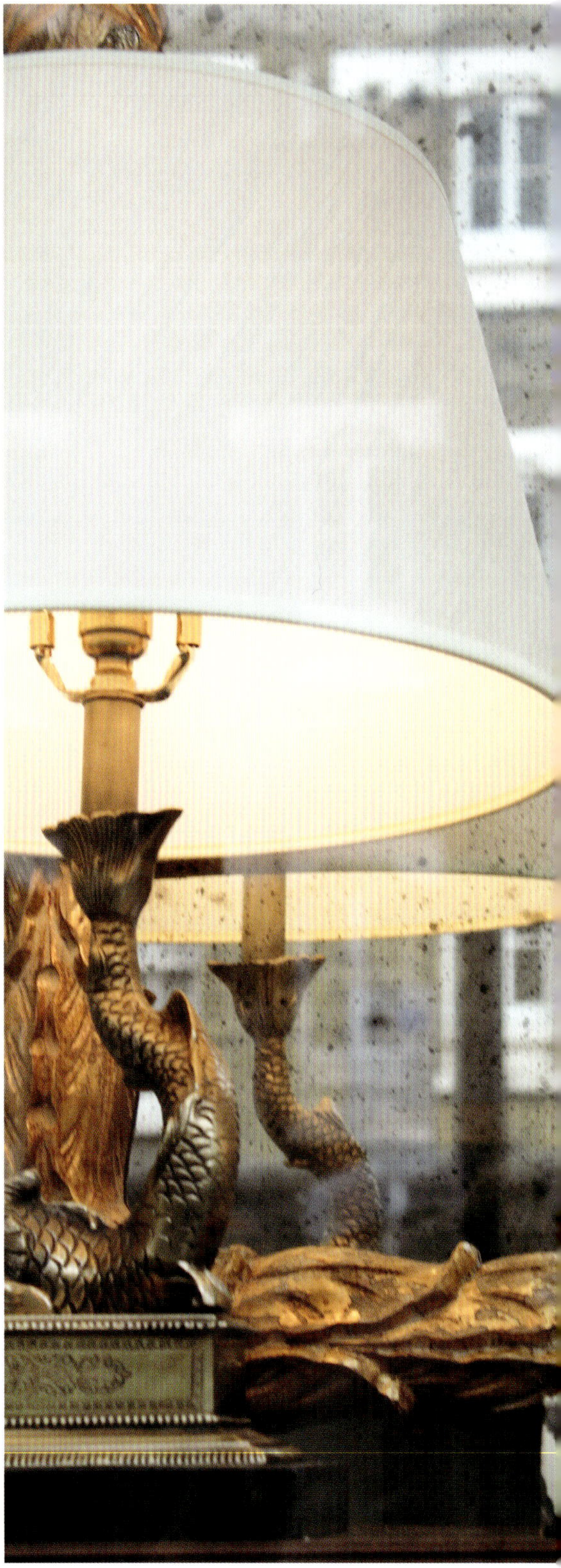

SILVER PLATE
MINI WINE
COOLER
£6.95

SILVER PLATE
"HOTEL WARE"
SUGAR BOWL
£8.95

PENTREATH & HALL Architect Ben Pentreath
and designer / collector Bridie Hall have joined
forces to create a petite boutique called Pentreath
& Hall in the heart of Bloomsbury, just off the
popular Lamb's Conduit Street. It's packed with
gorgeous products, from vintage Penguin classics
and design books to cushions, candles, maps,
prints and architectural items. They often expand
into a pop-up shop next door, which is reserved for
more 'serious' antiques.

17 Rugby Street, Bloomsbury, London.
www.pentreath-hall.com

ROBERT KIME A favourite of many designers,
Robert Kime has been inspiring both professionals
and amateurs for decades. His strength is unusual
antiques, but he also does a roaring trade in divine
lampshades, ottomans and antique textiles. HRH
Prince Charles is a fan—Robert Kime worked on
Clarence House.

121 Kensington Church Street, Kensington, London.
www.robertkime.com

THE OLD CINEMA IN CHISWICK The Old
Cinema in Chiswick is a collectors' mecca: an
enormous space filled to the brim with all kinds of
furniture. Once I spotted a beautiful faux-bamboo
armoire here—just exquisite. You never know
what you'll find. Lots of designers love this place.

160 Chiswick High Road, Chiswick, London.
www.theoldcinema.co.uk

SPECIALITY STORES

ALTEA GALLERY It's a habit of many travellers to look for vintage and antique maps of the places they've been, which serve as an elegant reminder of the travels over the years. Unfortunately, map stores are becoming increasingly difficult to locate as so many are closing down due to diminishing foot trade (and / or going online), which is why Altea Gallery is a real find. Set in the moneyed streets of Mayfair, where its grand maps look right at home, this store houses an impressive collection of not just antique maps, but also sea charts, atlases and globes dating back to 1477. Many of the maps are rare, but there are also affordable maps, which make great gifts. Each is backed by a certificate of authenticity, and they'll also give advice on collecting and investing in antique maps. Don't miss the permanent exhibition of old London maps and City of London plans and panoramas.

35 Saint George Street, Mayfair, London. alteagallery.com

ANYA HINDMARCH BESPOKE Utterly unique, this wonderfully retro space is kitted out with vintage shop fittings and antique display cases: the perfect backdrop for Anya Hindmarch's bespoke workshop. Choose from Anya's gorgeous range of bags, and then watch the craftsmen working on monograms before your eyes. The personalised Walton weekend bag is the current bestseller.

15–17 Pont Street, Knightsbridge, London. www.anyahindmarch.com

Opposite *Berry Brothers and Rudd*
This page from left to right *Anya Hindmarch;*
Lock & Co.; creative window displays in Soho
Following pages *More creativity on Columbia Road*

BERRY BROTHERS AND RUDD The oldest wine and spirit merchant in London, dating from 1698, this very handsome and very dignified place is a must-see for oenophiles and history fans. It's long been known as the kind of place where you make a yearly appointment with one of the wine staff to talk about how many cases you'll need to restock all of your estates. (I have it on good authority that the Queen Mother used to replenish her supplies from here—although not personally, of course.) One friend says it's the kind of place you go to buy "posh plonk". However, there's another quirky side to the store. It owns a massive weighing scale that was originally used to weigh wine, spirits and coffee. As it was one of the few scales in London a century or so ago, it was also used to weigh London's upper class, the measurements of which were hidden in a 19th-century ledger. Beau Brummell and Lord Byron were regularly weighed in here. Look closely at it (ask a member of staff to see it), and you'll see a few familiar names! There's also a legend about a secret underground passage that runs from the shop to St James's Palace. It supposedly dates from the Stuart era, when Merry Monarch Charles II would use it to slip across the road unnoticed into a high-class brothel. But less-than-kind critics have said that it might have been used for, er, alcoholic supplies going the other way. There is certainly a bricked-up archway in the basement pointing in the direction of Clarence House, but as for who bricked it and for what security reason, the discreet staff at Berry Brothers would never tell anyone that. All that's been revealed is that a Tudor well was discovered recently, but that's not quite as exciting as a secret tunnel.

3 St James's Street, Mayfair, London. www.bbr.com

BILL AMBERG Bill Amberg made his name making luxurious leather bags. Now he does everything from hide-covered walls and handrails to leather bars, desks and tables. Much of it is bespoke work for the likes of Aston Martin, Penguin, Alfred Dunhill and Selfridge, but individuals can also order custom-made bags, weekenders and cases.

2 Lonsdale Road, Queen's Park, London. www.billambergstudio.com

CECIL COURT Tucked beside the National Gallery, this is a quirky little Victorian thoroughfare filled with high-end print shops, antiquarian bookstores, maps and other interesting printed bits. It's a little like a scene out of Harry Potter. You half expect some wizard to be bent over inside one of the bookstores, nosing through a great big tome on some obscure subject. (In fact, the street is often used by film companies looking for an authentic Victorian street.) It's a great place for finding gifts, whether for yourself or your bookish friends, and particularly good for signed or first editions. They're not that expensive, either. David Drummond's theatre-related ephemera shop is also well worth a browse. Wander down here and see if you're not tempted to step inside one of the stores.

Cecil Court, Covent Garden, London.

CHLOE ALBERRY Set inside an eye-catching blue boutique on Portobello Road, Chloe Alberry specialises in door handles, cabinet fittings, hooks and mirrors. It's a great store to source unusual pieces for your doors and cabinetry. There's everything from cricket-ball door handles (used to great effect in many rooms in Firmdale Hotel's Dorset Square hotel), to heavy, Parisian-style gilt doorknockers. Everything you need to make an entrance. Or an exit.

84 Portobello Road, Notting Hill, London. www.chloealberry.com

DAYLESFORD ORGANIC has many fans, but others feel it's a little, well, like an idealised version of the countryside. Whatever you think about it, there's no doubt it has been successful in selling most of us the idea of a rural idyll. The main premise is that of a farm shop and café in the middle of the city, and the produce ranges are certainly delicious, if a little expensive. However, there's a side line in gardening gear and homewares that's perhaps more interesting. And during the Chelsea Flower Show, the Pimlico branch of Daylesford sets up a sweet shop promoting its gardenalia, which ranges from wellington boots to books, tools (all too beautiful to use in an actual garden!), and all manner of plant tags and pretty things. There are also locations in Notting Hill and elsewhere, including a grand farm shop in the Cotswolds.

44B Pimlico Road, Pimlico, London. www.daylesford.com

FALKINERS Falkiners specialises in bookbinding paper, such as Japanese chiyogami paper, and also runs bookbinding workshops—a must-do for those who love books and want to create something special of their own. (A lovely idea for a gift, especially if it's filled with photos of the recipient.)

76 Southampton Row, Victoria, London. www.falkiner.com

FLORIS The oldest family-owned perfumer in the world, Floris has been capturing beautiful scent since 1730. Its mahogany cases—made for the Great Exhibition of 1851—houses all the company's bestsellers, including Bouquet de la Reine, made to celebrate the marriage of Queen Victoria and Prince Albert. If some of the scents seem a bit dated, compared to the modern styles (although powdery florals are coming back with a vengeance), head to the rear of the boutique, where there's a bespoke perfume room, and also a museum of the history of the company. It's very interesting. Who knew that Ian Fleming (James Bond's creator) liked house blend No. 89? And mentioned Floris in many of his novels? Marilyn Monroe adored Floris Rose Geranium and ordered huge quantities to be shipped to her suite at the Beverly Hills Hotel. Don't miss a whiff of the Limes and White Rose—bliss!

89 Jermyn Street, Mayfair, London. www.florislondon.com

GREEN & STONE OF CHELSEA Green & Stone has been part of the King's Road streetscape for decades, and thankfully hasn't been edged out by the big chain stores that are muscling in on Chelsea's main shopping strip. It's one of the loveliest and most atmospheric places to purchase art supplies in London (the other is L. Cornelissen and Son), and no one bothers you, which is quite nice if you're the kind who likes to spend hours deliberating over pastel colours, paper and which pencils are better for sketching. There are all sorts of curiosities here, from unusual art supplies to unique gifts. But perhaps the most charming part is the store itself: sloping worn floorboards, old map chests, gorgeous antique shelving and drawers … the perfect backdrop for such creative bits and pieces.

259 King's Road, Chelsea, London. www.greenandstone.com

*From **opposite left to right** Cecil Court; Daylesford Organic; Chloe Alberry*
*Following **pages from left to right** Pastels in all shades of blue at L.Cornelissen and Son; Lacy Gallery*

162 **LABOUR AND WAIT** Well known among the minimalist sector of the design crowd, Labour and Wait offer a wonderfully stylish, delightfully pared-back take on household items. You can't miss the store—the shiny, tiled, British-racing-green storefront is as eye-catching as the simple but smart black typography of the signs—but once you're past the façade your attention will be well and truly on the products inside. There are lots of 'timeless, functional products for daily life' here, as Labour and Wait puts it, which have been reimagined for the modern user. In fact, the whole store feels a little like a small, old-fashioned general store reinvented for the hipster age. They also sell their merchandise at Dover Street Market in Mayfair, but this place is a better place to shop for things you never knew you needed.

18 Cheshire Street, Bethnal Green, London. www.labourandwait.co.uk

LACY GALLERY There are not enough superlatives to describe this incredible place, which may only sell antique and period picture frames but is a work of art in itself. There are three crowded but glorious floors of frames here, more than 1000 in total, ranging from Edwardian and Victorian to 18th century. Most have come from estates and museums (some are inevitably damaged), but stock is sourced from all over Europe, and all are worthy of hanging on their own, without even a picture inside them. The store restores frames and then sells them back to museums, dealers, collectors and artists, as well as hiring them out for fashion shoots and films. They can restore, re-gild, mount or fit your own frames and images, but it's more fun to come here and browse the stock, which is stacked on every wall and even hung in between each other to great effect.

203 Westbourne Grove, Notting Hill, London. www.lacygallery.co.uk

LASSCO Lassco is a firm favourite with decorators, interior designers and DIY builders looking for unusual pieces to embellish their home (or their clients' homes). It's an architectural salvage space tucked under the arches in Bermondsey, which has become well known for offering all kinds of design treasures, from period doors and French windows to old bath-tubs and staircases, right down to the smaller stuff, such as doorknobs. There's also a café and a bakery. There is another location at Brunswick House, which has a fabulous restaurant attached to it.

41 Maltby Street, Bermondsey, London. www.lassco.co.uk

L. CORNELISSEN AND SON If you're an artist, this is going to be a London highlight. This historic, 100-year-old art store is filled with antique signage, and original timber cabinetry and panelling, complete with gilded numbers; all just as beautiful as the paints stored within them. There are all sorts of irresistible pigments here, as well as beautiful brushes, paper and other inspiring things. All the artistic greats have bought their bits here. Don't miss the antique drawers full of coloured pastels at the back: you'll want to start drawing even if you don't know how. Or you could just look at the cabinetry and be enthralled.

105 Great Russell Street, Bloomsbury, London. www.cornelissen.com

LOCK & CO. Lock & Co. has been part of the Mayfair landscape for decades. It's a wonderfully old-school shop in St James's Street (a panama's throw from St James's Palace) that features one of the finest examples of an early-18th-century shopfront in London. This is where the rich, wealthy and famous have always purchased their toppers. Head measurements are kept a secret, but the boxes are displayed in a beautiful way, like a millinery 'still life' in the front salon. One of the company's newest clients, the Duchess of Cambridge, sources much of her stylish headwear here.

6 St James's Street, Mayfair, London. www.lockhatters.co.uk

MAGGIE OWEN Gorgeous shopfront; gorgeous jewellery; gorgeous person! This cobalt-blue boutique is surely one of the most photographic boutiques in London. It's a former dairy—London's first dairy, in fact—that's been converted without losing any of the old tiles and lettering. But then, Maggie Owen clearly knows a thing or two about handling precious materials. Her jewellery collections are poetic, beautiful poems to the qualities of gold, silver and all kinds of metals and stones. There are glam necklaces that are dramatic enough for the opera, subtle numbers that speak of first dates, and everything in between. And none of it is expensive. In fact, everything looks prohibitive in price, but it's not at all.

13 Rugby Street, Bloomsbury, London. www.maggieowen.com

Opposite A vintage book of patterns on Portobello Road
Following pages from left to right *A window display by Cadogan Estates in Mayfair; Maggie Owen*

PURDEY GUN & RIFLE MAKERS If you or your other half is a fan of sporting guns, then a visit to Mayfair and one of its esteemed gun showrooms, Purdey Gun & Rifle Makers, might excite. Purdey have been bought by a French luxury-goods conglomerate—Richemont—but their appeal remains undiminished. Purdey's showroom is worthwhile to visit, if only because of its famous Long Room, where great shots from the past two centuries have been fitted for their guns. The firm has enjoyed royal patronage since 1838, when Queen Victoria placed her first order, for a pair of pistols, while King Edward VII granted the first official Royal Warrant to the founder's son, James Purdey the Younger, in 1868. Even today, it still boasts clients from the British royal family. If you have time, make an appointment to see the legendary Long Room, with its glorious history and museum-quality pieces. A little secret: some of the D-Day Invasion was planned here, when Eisenhower's Deputy Chief of Staff, General Bedell-Smith, used the Long Room for battle planning in 1942. (General Eisenhower was also often at these meetings.) Even if you're not into sporting guns, the craftsmanship of the pieces here will astound you. Definitely worth a quick visit even if you don't have the US$100K+ for a bespoke rifle.

Audley House, 57–58 South Audley Street, Mayfair, London.
www.purdey.com

THE PORTOBELLO PRINT AND MAP SHOP A wonderful selection of reasonably priced antique botanical prints and maps.

109 Portobello Road, Notting Hill, London. www.portobelloprintandmap.uk

THE WYVERN BINDERY What a wondrous place this is! One of London's last remaining bookbinders, this workshop is an enthralling, atmospheric space filled with samples of leather, moleskins, papers and gold leaf, and young apprentices working on one-off commissions, limited editions and other bespoke orders. As well as books, they produce bespoke boxes, slipcases, portfolios, albums and props for film sets. (*Sherlock Holmes* and *Harry Potter* have been two.) They also repair antique books. A beautiful, beautiful store filled with the kind of books we've almost forgotten about.

56–58 Clerkenwell Road, Clerkenwell, London. www.wyvernbindery.com

THOMAS GOODE Thomas Goode sells beautiful British porcelain that's fit for the Queen, which is good because she often buys it—the store holds two warrants to supply the royal household. This is a magnificent Victorian showroom that is arguably one of London's foremost china, silverware, glass and luxury tableware emporiums. It is so entrancing that people come here just to wander the displays and dream of the dinnerware. It carries most of the world's most respected heritage brands

along with many cutting-edge contemporary designs, but it's usually the more traditional designs that draw people in, especially the botanical collections. There's glass and crystalware by Saint-Louis and Venini, and silverware and cutlery by Puiforcat, Odiot and Christofle, and much more. A note of warning: Even if you're not remotely interested in dinnerware or pretty plates, your eyes will start to sparkle after a few minutes here.

17-22 South Audley Street, Mayfair, London. www.thomasgoode.com

W SITCH AND CO W Sitch is a family-run business set up in 1776, specialising in the reproduction and restoration of metal light fittings. It's housed in a wonderfully atmospheric, old-fashioned (I mean, authentically old-fashioned!) old store in Soho, spread over three rickety floors filled to the rafters with period lighting. Everything here is beautiful, even the cracked old gold lanterns. There are some enormous pieces; it's not surprising that W Sitch supplied the light fittings for the film *Titanic*. It also looks after the wall brackets that grace the state dining room at No. 10. For the rest of us, W Sitch will repair, rewire and repolish most period lights or convert a favourite vase into a lamp. Don't miss the room out the back, where an elderly gentleman has been restoring lights for decades.

48 Berwick Street, Soho, London. www.wsitch.co.uk

ZUBER The word 'Zuber' is enough to evoke a sigh into many design lovers. It's a French wallpaper company that still uses the old block printing method to do elaborate and intricate wallpapers. They're so beautiful, many people just buy one roll and create a folding screen from them. There are French garden settings, scenes from colonial days in the Far East, and, of course, period scenes from 19th-century England.

67 Pimlico Road, Pimlico, London. www.zuber.fr

Opposite from left to right *W Sitch and Co; Zuber*
Above *The façade of the artshop Green and Stone*

BROMPTON DESIGN QUARTER A bit of a loose term for a neighbourhood with lots of lovely design shops, this tag has nonetheless been effective in drawing people away from King's Road and into this cloistered corner of South Kensington. There are now many fine design and fashion stores here, including one of the first places to arrive on the scene, Michelin House on Fulham Road, which encompasses a furniture store and the restaurant Bibendum. The neighbourhood really hit its sartorial stride in the late 1990s when big brands such as Chanel moved in. Some lament that the 'old' BC (Brompton Cross) has gone now that the double Cs (Coco Chanel) and other shiny names have moved in; others say it's as good as it always was. One thing is for certain: several stores have closed and there is a different atmosphere to the place. Not bad; just different. New arrivals include both Carven (that now-cult Paris fashion label) and 3.1 Phillip Lim, which have opened up their first UK stores on Pelham Street, running off the Brompton Cross intersection, joining Kenzo and Acne's fashion boutique, which opened up its second UK store back in August. J. Crew's more premium collection also has a store here. In fact, Pelham Street now feels very contemporary and almost 'edgy' in style. On Fulham Road, the main thoroughfare through Brompton Cross, there's Ralph Lauren (amazing store), Stella McCartney (fashion), Butler and Wilson (beautiful vintage jewellery and gowns), Theo Fennell (jewellery), Isis (a fav with the 30-somethings) and Joseph right in the centre of the village. Around the corner, on Drycott Avenue and Walton Street, there are more stores, including Jil Sander, Melissa Odasbash Swimwear, Marie-Chantal, and Andrew Martin antiques. There are far too many to name, so the best thing to do is start at the southern end of Fulham Road (say, at Sumner Place) and wander slowly north-east until you get to the Bibendum building in the middle of the village (don't worry; you'll see it from a distance!). From there, you can peel off to Pelham Street, Draycott Avenue, Walton Street or just keep going. (Fulham Road becomes Brompton Road at that point.)

HOUSE OF HACKNEY House of Hackney's famous palm-tree print has been all over the internet, having been seen everywhere from orangeries in Marrakech to sunrooms in LA. But there are other House of Hackney prints that are just as gorgeous, and just as bright. There are also clothes, shoes and accessories, all arranged in brilliant fashion in its townhouse-style flagship store. There is a small collection in Liberty, too.

131 Shoreditch High Street, London. www.houseofhackney.com

Clockwise from top left Nicholas Haslam; Ralph Lauren; House of Hackney
Following pages from left to right *Bibendum restaurant; St Paul's art studios*

Right *Display at Soane Britain*

172 MARIANNA KENNEDY Marianna Kennedy is renowned for her brightly colored resin lamps, blue-and-pink Mercury mirrors and lovely little lacquer tables.
3 Fournier Street, Spitalfields, London. www.mariannakennedy.com

NICHOLAS HASLAM / DAVID LINLEY The Nicholas Haslam design store in Belgravia has been a mecca for interior design lovers and those seeking interior design solutions for decades. Now owned and managed by Paolo Moschino (Nicholas's former business partner) and Philip Vergeylen, it's one of the most stylish stores on this corner. Another is David Linley, the furniture and design store owned by Princess Margaret's son, an immensely talented designer. Both are worth a look for their grace, beauty and inspiration.
Nicholas Haslam: 202 Ebury Street, Belgravia, London.
www.nicholashaslam.com;
David Linley: 60 Pimlico Road, Belgravia, London. www.david linley.com

RALPH LAUREN We all know how expensive Ralph Lauren's collections and stores are, but they are so incredibly beautiful, we tend to wander in anyway. The thing is, they offer great inspiration, whether you're a professional designer or an amateur looking for ideas on how to achieve that certain kind of elegance that Mr Lauren and his team do so well. This Brompton Cross store is one of the loveliest Ralph Lauren Home stores in the world, next to the one in Beverly Hills and of course the flagship in New York's Upper East Side. There's everything from silverware to bedding here, but it's the way it's all laid out that makes for a beautiful education. Come here for a lesson in sophistication. (The Bond Street store is also an education in style.)
105 Fulham Road, South Kensington, London;
1 New Bond Street, Mayfair, London. www.ralphlauren.com

SOANE BRITAIN Soane's owner Lulu Lytle is amazing example of what you can do if you set your mind to it. She opened her now-legendary store in order to sell unusual furniture and pieces. When she realised that many of Britain's craftspeople and small companies were closing down, she started investing in them. In 2011, she bought the Leicestershire rattan company where her designs were made, and is now designing special 'Soane' pieces with them to sell in her store, as well as bespoke furniture. (The woven-rattan bar at the Chiltern Firehouse is one.) She has invested in others, too. As a result, she is now commissioning bespoke pieces that are for sale in Soane, alongside other furniture she sources; all beautifully displayed in her spacious but inviting Pimlico store.
50–52 Pimlico Road, Chelsea, London. www.soane.co.uk

TIMOROUS BEASTIE In the last year or so, this name has cropped up everywhere, particularly on blogs where design fans rave about the wallpaper. Founded by two Glasgow School of Art students, it's a design form that specialises, as you'd guess by the quirky name, in elaborate prints. Their speciality is wallpaper, but it's not like most wallpaper we know today. For instance, the *toile de jouy* is, if you look up close, a scene of modern-day Scotland. And the Grand Blotch Damask is more like a modern painter than a French Rococo. The designs can now be found in the V&A boardroom and Claridge's, and the company has collaborated with Liberty, Fornum & Mason and Philip Treacy to produce bespoke prints.

46 Amwell Street, Islington, London. www.timorousbeasties.com

THE CONRAN SHOP Sir Terence Conran has been part of the London design scene for decades now, and this store is still one of the best for ideas, inspiration and design. It's located in the gloriously ornate 1911 Art Deco Michelin Building that was once the HQ for the great tyre company, and the exterior has been left mostly as it was, complete with green and white tiles and iconic Michelin sign. Inside, it's a different story; there's modern, innovative furniture, dreamy lights, bold accessories and ideas galore. It's not all contemporary; there are also one-off vintage pieces and a few classics. Don't miss a bowl of oysters in the oyster bar. Or a full meal in the famous Bibendum restaurant.

81 Fulham Road, Brompton Cross, London. www.conranshop.co.uk

Opposite *The shop at Bluebird*
This page from left to right *A detail of the staircase at Ralph Lauren's flagship store; interior of Soane Britain*
Following pages from left to right *Kate Spade's window design; floral street art on King's Road in Chelsea*

THE NEW CRAFTSMEN The New Craftsmen taps into the current mania for handmade things. Many of us, perhaps in retaliation of all things electronic, switched-on and internet-y, are trying to switch off by doing embroidery, knitting, painting, watercolours, photography, sewing and well, anything that doesn't involve a keyboard. And now there is a shop where such objects are beautifully displayed in a contemporary way. Originally a pop-up shop in Mayfair, it is now a permanent store in a stunning Arts and Crafts building that was formerly workshop for makers of leather breeches (how very fitting). The collections range from glassware and ceramics to books and textiles, all drawn from 75 makers from across the country.

34 North Row, Mayfair, London, W1. www.thenewcraftsmen.com

THE SHOP AT BLUEBIRD This Grade II–listed building began life as an Art Deco garage complex built for the Bluebird Motor Company in 1923. At the time, the garages were among the largest in Europe, with room for 300 cars and a further 650 square metres (7000 square feet) was given over to workshops. On either side of the garage, two further buildings contained lounges segregated into spaces for ladies, owners and chauffeurs. Fast forward to 1997 and Sir Terence Conran's Conran Group took over the building, converting the old showroom into the Bluebird Gastrodrome, a mixed-use business combining a restaurant, bar, café and private dining rooms. It's still a vast space, so it may feel off-putting, but venture in, because there is a great deal to discover here. The retail store sells high-end designer fashions, art books and upmarket homewares, but it's the fashion that is particularly fabulous, with collections from Marni, Chloé, Carven, and Isabel Marant, as well as up-and-coming labels. Don't miss its fantastic range of accessories either, ranging from bags and books to candles. Some people do complain that the price tags will make your eyes water (£600 seems to be an average figure here!), but the browsing is free. So make yourself at home: there's a lot to see.

350 King's Road, Chelsea, London. www.theshopatbluebird.com

FASHION

11 BOUNDARY 11 Boundary is a bright Shoreditch boutique selling contemporary labels including By Malene Birger, Winter Kate and accessories from Tom Ford and House of Harlow.

11 Boundary Street, Shoreditch, London. www.11boundary.com

A LA MODE Josephine Turner has been sourcing stylish fashion for her equally stylish store just off Sloane Square for decades now, and shows no sign of slowing down or losing her innate good taste. There are pieces from Nina Ricci, Vionnet, Giambattista Valli and Oscar de la Renta as well as home-grown labels.

10 Symons Street, Chelsea, London. www.alamodefashion.co.uk

AIMÉ The sisters Val and Vanda Heng Vong opened Aimé in 1999 when they couldn't source their favourite French labels in London. The pair still import French labels (Isabel Marant, APC) along with Italian labels such as Forte Forte and Faliero Sarti. There's another branch in Shoreditch.

32 Ledbury Road, Notting Hill, London. www.aimelondon.com

Opposite *Display at Ralph Lauren*
Above *Detail of fashion at Joseph*

ALEXANDER WANG Some shoppers may be a little perplexed at this store. Where are the clothes? The change rooms? Even the rails? It's very pared back, austere and hard edged, but that's the point. Fashion designer Alexander Wang is renowned for his fiercely unfrivolous fashion. And so naturally he called upon fellow minimalist Vincent Van Duysen to design his first standalone location in Europe—a 622-square-metre (6700-square-foot) outpost in a former Mayfair post office. With its concrete floors, stainless-steel wall panels, and chrome display rails, the interior nods to Wang's hard-edged but oh-so-handsome fashions. Magnificent. In every way.

43/44 Albemarle Street, Mayfair, London. www.alexanderwang.com

BALMAIN French fashion house Balmain has opened a London outpost in a ravishing store designed by architect Joseph Dirand. It's a combination of Queen Anne style and classic French elegance, with a stately fireplace, parquet-like stone floors, and a profusion of mouldings. All very French. All very Balmian. And the clothes? They're as beautiful as always. But the store is worth a look for the interior alone.

69 South Audley Street, Mayfair, London. www.balmain.com

BROWNS This legendary store is famed for its first-class collection of international labels, which ranges from Dolce & Gabbana to Valentino to the more cutting-edge names. And don't miss the sister store, Browns Labels for Less.

24–27 South Molton Street, Mayfair, London. www.brownsfashion.com

BY MARLENE BIRGER Danish fashion designer Marlene Birger started her successful career in 1997 with the label Day Birger et Mikkelson, co-founded with Keld Mikkelsen, which was celebrated worldwide for its clean lines and fresh, contemporary look. It was edgy but still classic—very Danish, in fact. Then she set up her own independent label in 2003, brought out several books about her beautiful clothes and homes, and the 'cult' of Marlene was really complete. She then moved to London, retaining a holiday home on Mallorca, and left the position as creative director in January 2014, although the label still bears all the signatures of her designs. She now runs the interior design company Birger1962, but you can still look like her with a piece or two from this boutique. India Hicks is just one fan of her sexy but understated numbers, which are elegant enough for business but swap easily to night-time events with an accessory or three.

28–29 Marylebone High Street, Marylebone, London.

www.bymarlenebirger.com

CELINE This store's interior of marble tiles (all 6000 of them) is stunning, but it palls in beauty to the clothes, which, under Phoebe Philo, are pure class. Try not to be distracted by the modern-day beds and the huge brass lights that spread out over the central atrium, both designed by the Dutch artist Thomas Poulsen, and just focus on the fashion. Focus, focus, focus!

103 Mount Street, Mayfair, London. www.celine.com

DIVERSE A die-hard Islington boutique, Diverse offers a one-stop shop with everything from Isabel Marant to Kenzo.

294 Upper Street, Islington, London. www.diverseclothing.com

DOVER STREET MARKET This Mayfair shopping mecca—really a six-storey temple to high style— was the idea of Comme des Garçons' Rei Kawakubo, who wanted to bring together the world's most desirable fashion labels in a series of flowing spaces. She also encouraged the merchandisers to create amazing displays to illustrate the collections. One memorable Alber Elbaz Lanvin display was an installation that recreated a room from the Hotel de Crillon in Paris, after it had survived an outrageously wild night of partying, complete with empty bottles of champagne and knocked-over glasses. A sexy gown and gentleman's attire were strewn around, and a mannequin positioned under the bed so that only her rear end was visible! That's the kind of drama you'll find here, at least in the rails! If you're patient and watchful, you can pick up

amazing pieces here; one regular customer snapped up a Valentino Prive ballgown reduced from £8000 to virtually nothing. Inspiring, innovative and quite possibly the most influential store in the world.

17–18 Dover Street, Mayfair, London. www.doverstreetmarket.com

DUKE STREET EMPORIUM This Mayfair newcomer is a sister store to the Shop at Bluebird. It has a similar style but with more of a focus on smaller, up-and-coming labels, such Maison Kitsuné.

55 Duke Street, Mayfair, London. www.dukestreetemporium.com

EGG Maureen Doherty's stylishly simple and utterly beguiling boutique in Knightsbridge has been open for more than a decade now, but fans still love wandering down the cute narrow side street and in the doors of this whitewashed former dairy to see what's on offer. Everything in Egg has a timelessness that means you can wear the clothes year after year. As well as the clothes, there are also hand-crafted household items, and linens; all very pick-upable! Doherty once worked with Japanese designer Issey Miyake and gave the famous author and ceramicist Edmund de Waal his first show, and you can see the influences of the two gentlemen in this store and its collections. Everything is simple, beautiful, and irresistible. It's difficult to create clothes that are classic and contemporary at the same time, but this place proves it can be done.

36 Kinnerton Street, Knightsbridge, London.. eggtrading.com

ERDEM Fans of fashion designer Erdem Moralioglu will be over the moon to know that he has opened his first standalone flagship in London's Mayfair neighborhood. Designed with his longtime partner, architectural designer Philip Joseph, the two-storey boutique is filled with vintage furnishings from local gallery Sigmar and a mix of moody paintings and witty drawings by Andy Warhol and Jean Cocteau. Oh, and Erdem's gorgeous clothes, of course.

70 S Audley Street, Mayfair, London. www.erdem.com

FEATHERS Originally set up in Kensington High Street in 1969, where it sold Ossie Clark and Bill Gibb, Feathers has decamped to Knightsbridge and is run by the second-generation retailers Peter and Suzanne Burstein, who buy labels including Rick Owens, Jil Sander and Rochas, plus home-grown talents such as Alexander McQueen.

42 Hans Crescent, Knightsbridge, London. www.feathersfashion.com

From opposite left to right *Textural fashion*
Following pages from left to right *Dover Street Market fashion; Chanel jacket detail; Joseph boxes*

Opposite *The famous timber mezzanine of Liberty department store*
Following pages from left to right *Temperley London; Ralph Lauren; Kate Spade*

184 **FLEUR B** The former fashion buyer Fleur Bird opened her first boutique in 2008 with her eponymous label, plus other equally stylish ones. The latter includes Victoria Beckham, Carven, Goat and 1970s-inspired dresses from Ellie Lines. There's an additional store in Duke Street.

8 Elystan Street, London. www.fleurb.co.uk

HEIDI KLEIN Heidi Klein has established a global reputation for slinky, sexy swimwear, which covers and compliments female bodies while still being seductive and comfy. This boutique is a whitewashed space that's designed to beautifully showcase the colourful costumes within it. It almost makes you feel as though you're already in a white villa in Greece, ready to dive into the deep, blue sea. As well as swimwear, there are gorgeous cover-ups and accessories, as well as rooms offering spray tans and other necessary holiday prep.

174 Westbourne Grove, Notting Hill, London. www.heidiklein.com

IRIS Founded by two friends, Annie Pollet and Sarah Claassen, Iris was launched with one store in Queen's Park in 2004 and has now branched out to four beautiful boutiques. The style of the fashion collections that Iris represents is decidedly feminine but easy to wear, and includes such names as Etoile by Isabel Marant and Vanessa Bruno. A great place to find pretty pieces.

73 Salisbury Road, Queens Park, London. 97 Northcote Road, and
129 Chiswick High Road, Chiswick, London. www.irisfashion.co.uk

JOSEPH Joseph remains one of London's most loved fashion boutiques for its impressive collections, among them Céline, Balenciaga and Lanvin, to name a few. There is also a Joseph collection, equally gorgeous.

315 Brompton Road, South Kensington, London. www.joseph-fashion.com

LARK LONDON Founded by the former model and merchandiser Phoebe Pring, this sweet Kensal Rise shop is the place to find chic separates from well-known labels, such Finders Keepers, as well as designers you might not have heard of, such as Haaning & Htoon.

52 Chamberlayne Road, Kensal Rise, London. www.larklondon.com

MATCHES Matches has become a fashion phenomenon. Its success is such that it has been the subject of academic theses for those studying the business of fashion in schools and universities. From a humble beginning, the company has grown to an internationally famous brand, and yet still only has a few stores to keep its success intact. Clever move, Matches. The key to its popularity is in the clever, always-interesting edit of desirable labels—on-trend but with a mix of classics too. There are pieces by Max Mara, Bottega Veneta and Dolce & Gabbana as well as edgier, more directional ensembles from the likes of Altuzarra and Issa (one of the Duchess of Cambridge's favourite labels). It was one of the first small fashion boutiques in London to offer an extensive mix of labels and it's still one of the best.

85 Ledbury Road, Notting Hill, London; 87 Marylebone High Street, Marylebone, London (and other stores). www.matchesfashion.com

PHILIP TREACY If you're a fan of beautiful hats and headware, you will have almost certainly heard of Mr Treacy. He's been popping toppers on the heads of celebritites and royals for many years now. The late Isabella Blow not only helped Treacy to launch his millinery career, but famously wore many of his hats herself. He has also designed hats for Alexander McQueen, Karl Lagerfeld at Chanel, Valentino, Ralph Lauren and Donna Karan. Sarah Jessica Parker wore one of his designs to the *Sex and the City* film premiere. Sixty-six hats designed by Treacy were worn at the royal wedding of Prince William and Catherine Middleton on 29 April 2011, including the controversial fascinator worn by Princess Beatrice of York. Treacy's Pimlico boutique is a gallery to these glamorous hats, with both haute couture and ready-to-wear available for sale. Whatever your budget, there's certain to be something to suit. (Although a warning: this is not really a gardening hat kinda place!)

69 Elizabeth Street, Belgravia, London. www.philiptreacy.co.uk

RELLIK This legendary vintage store is not only a haunt for many sartorial-conscious A-listers, from Kate Moss to Lady Gaga, it's also a brilliant combination of the collectable (Vivienne Westwood, Yohji Yamamoto, Ossie Clark) and the classic and / or affordable pieces. There are pieces from the 1970s through to the 1990s. It's all a bit like being in a messy attic, but that's why people adore it. The excitement is in the hunting.

8 Golborne Road, Notting Hill, London. www.relliklondon.co.uk

THE CROSS From the second Sam Robinson opened her colourful, bohemian boutique in 1996, it has been one of the city's most loved fashion hotspots. It's a gorgeous gallery of various labels, from velvet evening wear to jersey basics. There are similarly cute home accessories too.

141 Portland Road, Notting Hill, London. www.thecrossshop.co.uk

TRILOGY If there's a pair of jeans that's perfectly cut for you, the team at Trilogy will be sure to find it.

31 Duke of York Square, Chelsea, London. www.trilogystores.co.uk

186

VINTAGE COUTURE

ANNIE'S Annie's has been selling glam old frocks to the fashion set for decades now (Kate Moss is a big fan), and never gets old (no pun intended). Everything here is exquisite, from the silk gowns to the bias-cut frocks to the Edwardian tea dresses. Wedding dresses are a speciality, but the sexy lacy slips are also popular. There are vintage ribbons, trimmings, even swimsuits.

12 Camden Passage, Camden, London. www.anniesvintageclothing.co.uk

BUTLER & WILSON Butler & Wilson has two stores—South Molton Street in Mayfair (a stunning façade) and another tucked away in a quiet part of Fulham Road. Both are beautiful, but it's the Fulham Road store (which has been there since 1972) that feels more like you're exploring the attic of a very wealthy, very stylish aunt who's kept all her couture from the 1920s and said: "help yourself". Butler & Wilson actually began as a small stand at the Antiquarius Market on King's Road, Chelsea in 1969. Slowly, the business grew, and now offers both Butler & Wilson's own brand vintage-inspired jewellery alongside authentic pieces from the last seven decades. They also sell vintage fashion to complement the main business, and the gowns are often more amazing than the bling. However, most do go for the jewels: the stores feel like Aladdin's cave of sparkles, and trying to resist by standing outside and staring forlornly into the window displays is futile! Just go in and treat yourself!

20 South Molton Street, Mayfair, London; 89 Fulham Road, Chelsea, London. www.butlerandwilson.co.uk

CRISTOBAL Church Street is teeming with wonderful antiques dealers, but the jewel in the crown is this costume-jewellery specialist, which has been selling exquisite vintage pieces for the past three decades from some of the best names, including Trifari, Miriam Haskell and Stanley Hagler.

26 Church Street, Lisson Grove, London. www.cristobal.co.uk

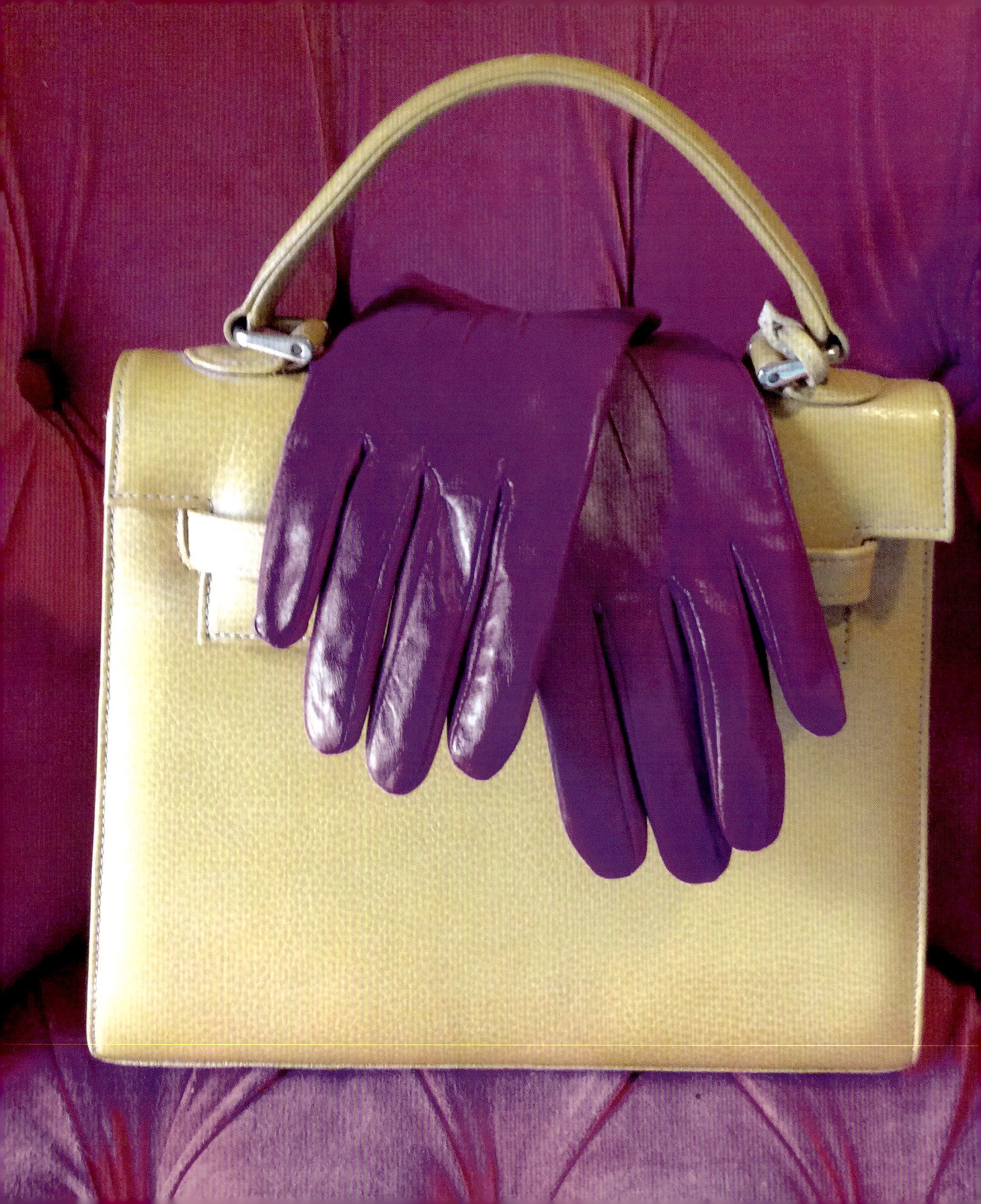

192 **CHARITY SHOPS** If you're after fashion bargains, especially when it comes to high-end design labels, your best bet is London's charity shops. These have long been the city's worst-kept secret for sourcing gorgeous, glamorous gowns, jackets, shoes and accessories (including bags). You'd be surprised by the quality of stock in these places. Many wealthy women shop for bargains in these boutiques, because the chances of unearthing an authentic Dior or Chanel for very cheap are actually quite high. Kate Moss and Sienna Miller regularly pop into the Marylebone branch of Cancer Research UK, where the likes of Louboutin, Dior and Miu Miu can be unearthed among the more high street chains, while the Beckhams have been sighted giving their unwanteds to the British Red Cross in Chelsea. There are usually clusters of these treasure troves in the moneyed suburbs, where the wealthy locals cast off their once-worn bits and bobs. Rumour has it even Diana used to dump her unwanted stuff at the resale boutiques in Cheval Place. For top labels, try the British Red Cross in Chelsea—a good source of Max Mara, Vivienne Westwood and other luxe labels worn by Chelsea ladies (69–71 Old Church Street); Cancer Research UK for pristine Jigsaw, Burberry and Marlene Birger (24 Marylebone High Street); Oxfam right across the road for similar goodies (91 Marylebone High Street), and the Octavia Foundation for designer clobber plus a fantastic vintage book department with old Christie's catalogues and art periodicals (211 Brompton Road).

GRAY'S ANTIQUES Many shoppers wandering down Oxford Street aren't aware that this treasure trove of antiques stalls even exists. It's tricky to find—perhaps consult a map or your phone before you head out—and it's labyrinthine and not that well signposted, but that makes it all the more fun. There are stalls selling antique watches, fashion and jewellery, silverware, interesting vases and other pieces, and all manner of odd bits and bobs. It's also a great place to get away from the general stress of Oxford Street.

58 Davies Street, Mayfair, London. www.graysantiques.com

PANDORA'S Pandora's is a veritable treasure trove of gorgeousness. It's a large store that's somehow gone under the radar of fashion peeps for many years, although a great many savvy shoppers (and stylists) do come here to search for stylish bargains. It's tucked away in a little street called Cheval Place, which has several of these vintage and resale / consignment stores on it, but Pandora's is by far the largest and the best. Much of the stuff comes from wealthy women who no longer have a need for their Chanels and Diors and other French pieces, but there are also a great many pieces that are clearly unworn, with the price tag still attached. These, I'm told, come from wealthy Middle Eastern princesses and other women who buy items and then decide they no longer like them. Everything is well organised into 'summer', 'winter', 'evening' and so on, with the labels carefully displayed. (All the Chanel is on one rail.) You do need time to sort through it all, but there are some amazing bargains to be had.

16–22 Cheval Place, Knightsbridge , London. www.pandoradressagency.com

THE EXCHANGE The Exchange is a somewhat pedestrian name for a store that is remarkably high end. Set on Gloucester Road, it's a stylish place that looks more like a Chelsea or Mayfair boutique than a consignment store, and that's exactly what the owners intended. Sure, it might specialise in vintage and 'gently worn' couture and designer labels, but it doesn't look like most second-hand stores. In fact, you'd be hard-pressed to guess what it is from the handsome black exterior. Inside, there are rails and rails of shiny sequined gowns, gorgeous beaded dresses, smart fitted blazers and coats (including Chanel and Max Mara), lovely scarves and shoes (oh, the shoes!), and everything in between, from classic white shirts to sassy skirts and party dresses. There's a second level downstairs, where the evening gowns are displayed, but honestly, the best bits are at street level. But you do need to be quick, especially when unworn Chanel heels are on offer for a mere £100.

72 Gloucester Road, South Kensington, London. www.theexchangelondon.com

VINTAGE FASHION, TEXTILES AND ACCESSORIES FAIR The vintage fashion, textiles and accessories fair at Hammersmith Town Hall is a big deal for those who love finding beautiful old couture or unusual pieces.

www.pa-antiques.co.uk

Previous pages *Bags and Chanel couture from The Exchange on Gloucester Road*
Opposite *Dresses on display at Butler & Wilson*

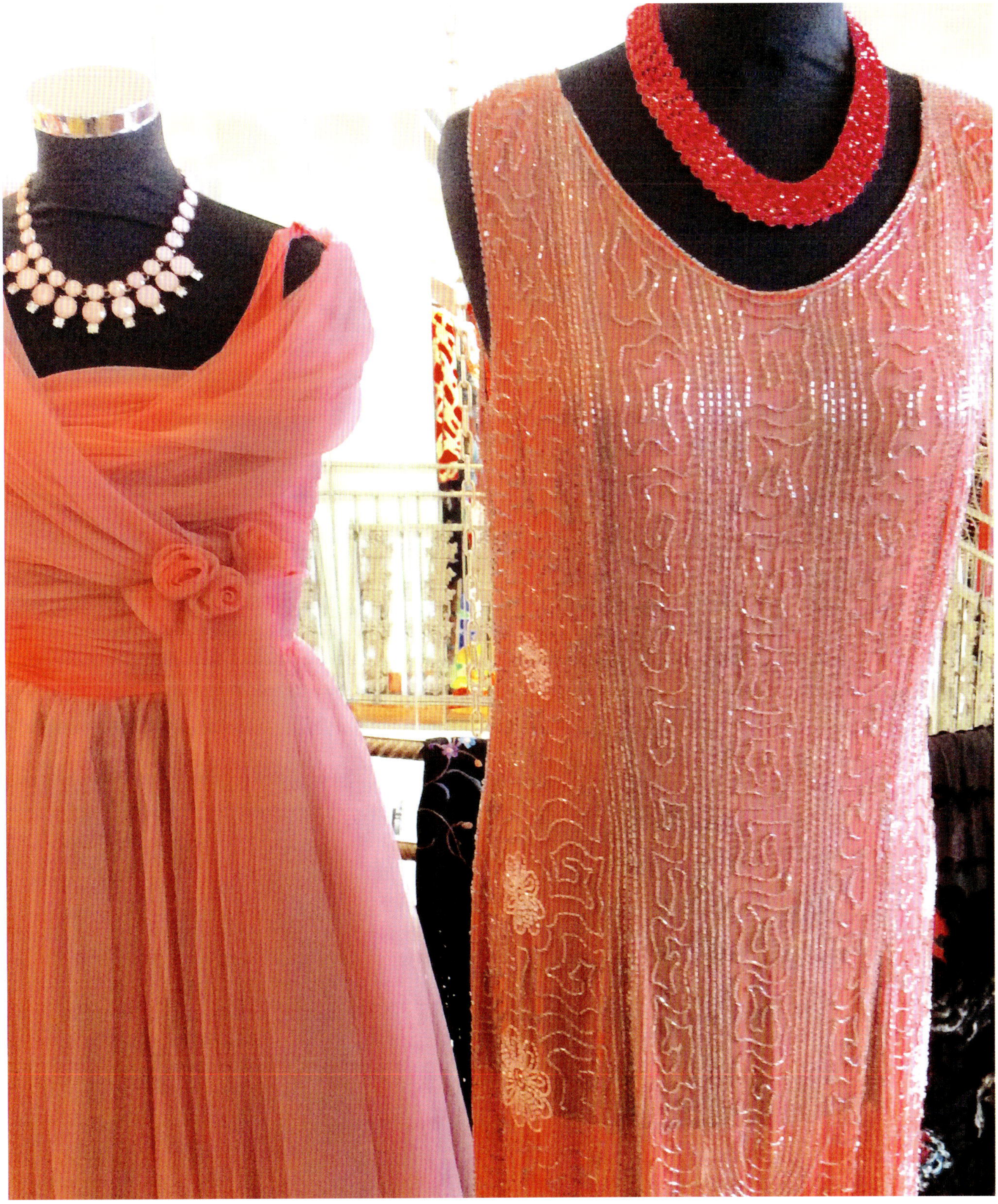

WILLIAM VINTAGE *Vogue* magazine called William Banks-Blaney "The Vintage King", and it might be right. This is one of the best places in the world to source beautiful, glamorous vintage couture and fashion, next to Didier Ludot in Paris and a few LA stores. Loved by stylists, fashion editors, actresses, TV personalities, and other aesthetes and fans of one-off fashion pieces, it's a superb source of pristine golden-age haute couture. There's everything from ruffled Yves Saint Laurent taffeta shirts to black Lanvin evening gowns to 1920 beaded chiffon dresses. At the time of writing this book, there was a glam YSL cape with feathered neckline, a hot pink Dior tea coat from 1963, a navy Halston evening frock in swirly chiffon (very Hollywood!), and a long navy Chanel tea coat-and-dress ensemble that had sadly been sold. Categories are sorted into 'LBD', 'Cocktail Hour', 'Black Tie', 'Boardroom', 'Ladies Days', 'Winter Chill', 'Poolside Scandal', and 'Haute Couture'. But for all the glamour and hype of William Vintage, prices are very reasonable. And he also has an online store, for when you can't get to London.

2 Marylebone Street, Marylebone, London. www.williamvintage.com

Opposite and above *Jacket detail and French cuffs at The Exchange*

ACKNOWLEDGMENTS

It has long been a dream of mine to do an illustrated guidebook to London, a city that I have loved for many years. London was not only my home for five years in the 1990s, it has also been a home away from home for the past five years. Whenever I land at Heathrow, I feel my spirits lift. Even the long wait at Immigration doesn't dampen my mood! Because I know that when I hop into a black cab, the driver will be unfailingly courteous and pleasant; when I check in at my preferred hotels (The Pelham or Blakes if I can afford it; High Road House if I can't), the staff will be warm and kind; when I step out into the streets and drop by the local stores for newspapers and supplies, the locals will full of humour and wit, and when I catch up with friends, they will always be happy and funny, and full of great stories of this always-interesting, always-memorable city.

And so I'd like to thank all those Londoners, for their kindness and warmth and wit. You are what makes London lovely.

I'd also like to thank Paul Latham and Joe Boschetti at Images Publishing for commissioning this book. Paul is my former boss, and we have done many books together. Joe is my dear friend, and is it he who believed in this project, and persuaded Paul to take it on. Both of them are gentlemen. Any author would be fortunate to have them onside. Thanks also to the rest of the team at IMAGES, particularly my editor, Gina Tsarouhas, the designer, Nikki Boehringer, Rod Gilbert, and Margit Dittes for pre-press.

Most importantly, I'd like to thank you, the reader—for buying this book. I hope it offers lots of ideas and inspiration for your next trip to London. For more information, feel free to follow me on Instagram at www.instagram.com/janellemcculloch_author.

London –
An Overview

● *Bridges*

  1 Lambeth Bridge
  2 Westminster Bridge
  3 Hungerford Bridge and Golden Jubilee Bridges
  4 Waterloo Bridge
  5 Blackfriar Bridge
  6 Millennium Bridge
  7 Southwark Bridge
  8 London Bridge
  9 Tower Bridge

● *Landmarks*

Kensal Green

Notting Hill

Kensin
Gard

Holland Park

Kensington

Hammersmith

Fulham

Chiswick

Royal Botanic
Gardens, Kew

River Thames

Richmond

Richmond Park

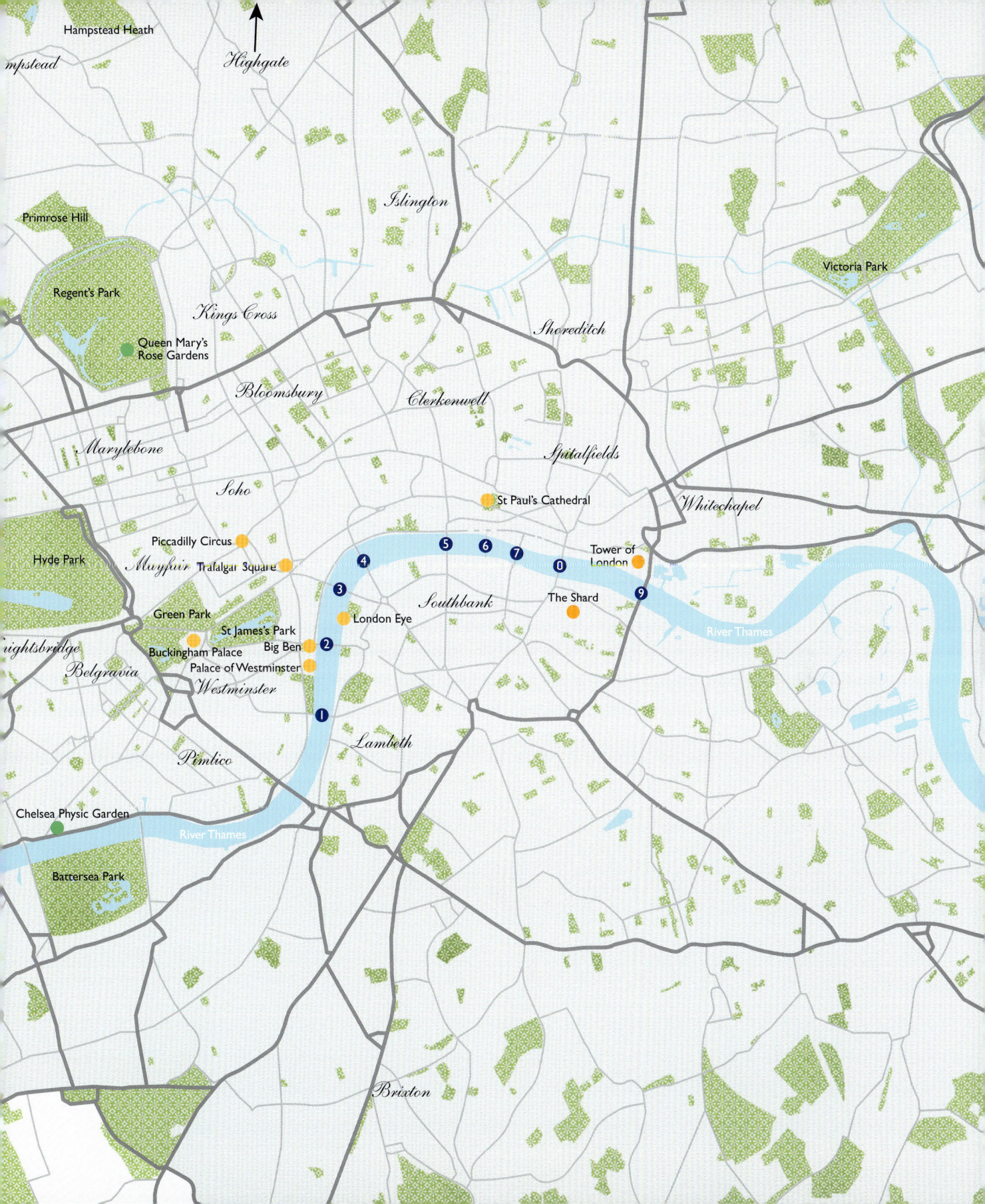

Hampstead Heath

Highgate

mpstead

Primrose Hill

Regent's Park

Queen Mary's
Rose Gardens

Islington

Victoria Park

Kings Cross

Shoreditch

Bloomsbury

Clerkenwell

Marylebone

Spitalfields

Soho

Whitechapel

St Paul's Cathedral

Hyde Park

Piccadilly Circus

Mayfair   Trafalgar Square

5   6   7

Tower of
London

4

0

Green Park

3

Southbank

The Shard

River Thames

St James's Park

London Eye

9

Buckingham Palace

Big Ben

2

ightsbridge

Belgravia

Palace of Westminster

Westminster

1

Pimlico

Lambeth

Chelsea Physic Garden

River Thames

Battersea Park

Brixton

203